ALASKA
TOTEM
POLES

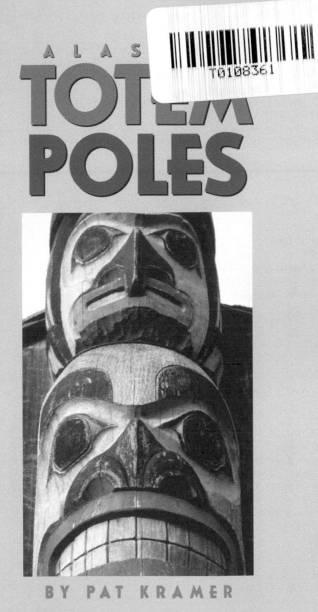

BY PAT KRAMER

FOREWORD BY DAVID A. BOXLEY

To all totem pole carvers whose names are lost in time.

I'd like to acknowledge all Totem People, especially Frank L. Fulmer, Tlingit carver; David R. Boxley and Wayne Hewson, Tsimshian artisans from Metlakatla; and the many Native people throughout Alaska and British Columbia who have invited me to countless ceremonies and kindly explained their stories, dances, and traditions so that they might be recorded with respect and honor. Thank you to Sealaska Heritage Institute and the Alaska Native Language Center, as well as Richard Dauenhauer for assisting with tribal name pronunciation guides, and to Donald Gregory and Steve Henrikson for their helpful review.

Library of Congress Cataloging-in-Publication Data

Kramer, Pat.
  Alaska's totem poles / by Pat Kramer.
    p. cm.
Includes bibliographical references and index.
  ISBN 978-0-88240-731-9
  1. Totem poles—Alaska—History. 2. Indians of North America—Material culture—Alaska. 3. Indian wood-carving—Alaska—History. 4. Indians of North America—Alaska—Antiquities. 5. Alaska—Antiquities. I. Title.

E98.T65K73 2003
979.8004'9712 —dc22

             2003021338

Photo Captions: *Cover*—Eagle with rounded beak meets Raven. *Title page*—Haines totem pole.

Archival Photo Credits: *Title page image* © Alaska Division of Community and Business Development; *Page 26*, Mrs. Forrest Hunt photo, MSCUA, University of Washington Libraries, negative number NA3610; *Page 38*, Clarence Leroy Andrews photo, MSCUA, University of Washington Libraries, negative number NA2890; *Page 45*, Otto C. Schallerer photo, MSCUA, University of Washington Libraries, negative number NA3854.

Alaska Northwest Books®
An imprint of

GRAPHIC ARTS
BOOKS®

P.O. Box 56118
Portland, OR 97238-6118
(503) 254-5591

Editor: Ellen Harkins Wheat
Design: Constance Bollen, cb graphics; Jean Andrews
Map: Gray Mouse Graphics

CONTENTS

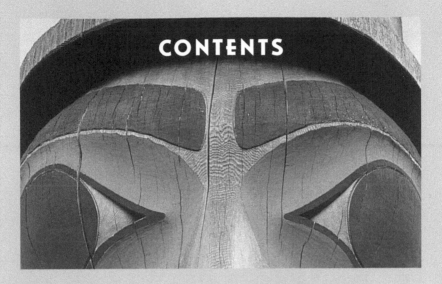

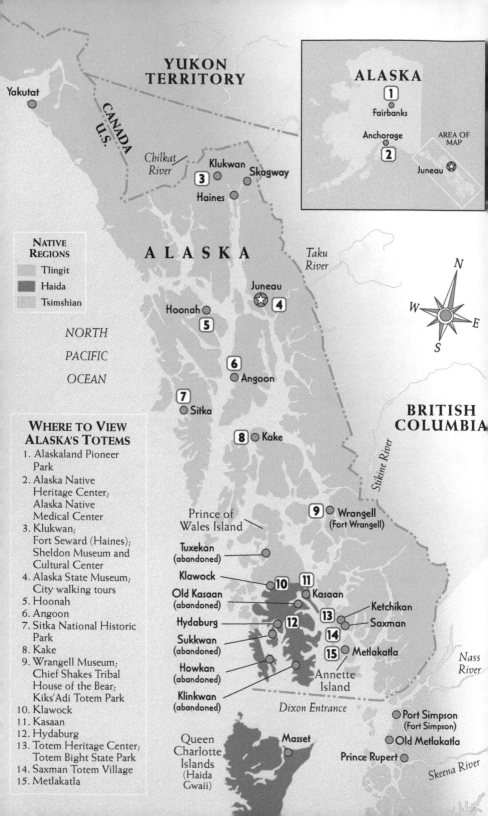

YUKON TERRITORY

ALASKA

☐1 Fairbanks

Anchorage
☐2

AREA OF MAP

Juneau ★

Yakutat

CANADA
U.S.

Chilkat River

Klukwan
☐3
Haines
Skagway

A L A S K A

Taku River

Juneau ★
☐4

Hoonah
☐5

NATIVE REGIONS

Tlingit
Haida
Tsimshian

NORTH

PACIFIC

OCEAN

☐6
Angoon

☐7
Sitka

☐8 Kake

BRITISH COLUMBIA

Stikine River

☐9 Wrangell (Fort Wrangell)

WHERE TO VIEW ALASKA'S TOTEMS

1. Alaskaland Pioneer Park
2. Alaska Native Heritage Center; Alaska Native Medical Center
3. Klukwan; Fort Seward (Haines); Sheldon Museum and Cultural Center
4. Alaska State Museum; City walking tours
5. Hoonah
6. Angoon
7. Sitka National Historic Park
8. Kake
9. Wrangell Museum; Chief Shakes Tribal House of the Bear; Kiks'Adi Totem Park
10. Klawock
11. Kasaan
12. Hydaburg
13. Totem Heritage Center; Totem Bight State Park
14. Saxman Totem Village
15. Metlakatla

Prince of Wales Island

Tuxekan (abandoned)

Klawock
Old Kasaan (abandoned)
☐10 ☐11 Kasaan

Hydaburg
☐12
Ketchikan
☐13
Saxman

Sukkwan (abandoned)
☐14

Howkan (abandoned)
☐15 Metlakatla
Annette Island

Klinkwan (abandoned)

Dixon Entrance

Nass River

Port Simpson (Fort Simpson)

Old Metlakatla

Queen Charlotte Islands (Haida Gwaii)

Masset

Prince Rupert

Skeena River

Foreword

Totem poles are the physical evidence, the touchable results of eons of Native history and tradition carried on in the songs and dances of our people. Even today in these modern times, they still matter.

Totem pole carvers, the artists who created these monuments, were the vessels by which the culture traveled. They had to be knowledgeable about oral history and carving styles. They were often called upon by distant villages and tribes to create works of art that would say to anyone who visited: this is who lives here. These are the stories, the history of this man, this clan, this village.

The arrival of non-Natives on theses shores brought many changes. The subsistence-based lifestyle was overrun by a wage-based existence, and the introduction of epidemic diseases and the influence of missionaries caused the disruption of the master/apprentice carver system. Native art, so close to and tied in with our cultural ceremonies, fell victim to the results of these extreme changes. Since the 1950s, though, the art has made a strong comeback. There are excellent carvers and culture bearers from all of the First Nations tribes leading and carrying on the art, language, and culture for the next generation.

Still, some things are hard to change . . . you would think that in these modern times, misconceptions and misinformation about Native people and totem poles would have been long ago "educated out" of non-Native people. Example: When I was a young boy I received a game for Christmas called "Fort Apache." It consisted of a number of plastic soldiers, Indians in various battle poses, a fort, teepees, cactus, and, of course, totem poles. Even though the Natives outside the Northwest Coast never had totem poles! Well, that was forty years ago, and it couldn't happen today . . . right? Recently I took some apprentices to Iowa to install a totem pole at a university in Dubuque. One of my companions, who knew of my Fort Apache story, purchased a plastic-wrapped toy for me in a gift shop there. It consisted of a cowboy, an Indian, and guess what? Yep, a totem pole.

So, I and others have been on this journey, as Native artists and culture bearers, hopefully to show that we as Northwest Native people are still here celebrating our culture, and creating these unique works of art. They are as important now as they were in the beginning.

As a carver, I spend weeks working on a cedar log to create a totem pole, whether it be for a Native or non-Native client. But each time that pole is raised, it is such an amazing, emotional experience. It makes me feel so connected. So fortunate to be a Native artist, having the opportunity to make a positive contribution.

Totem poles are so much more than carved cedar. They literally stand for who we are.

—David A. Boxley
Metlakatla, Alaska, and Kingston, Washington

1

An Introduction to Alaska's Totems

As travelers leave Seattle and Puget Sound and head north toward Alaska, they sail up the Inside Passage, through the deeply etched channels, bays, and fjords of coastal British Columbia and the Alaska Panhandle, also known as Southeast Alaska. This navigable edge of North America is exceptionally beautiful, with snowcapped mountains, rain-soaked cedar forests, and majestic glaciers spilling into the sea. On the journey, as travelers scan the shoreline, clusters of aged totem poles occasionally appear, looming in the mist. Calling silently to the eagles and ravens diving overhead, their soaring presence seems to symbolize something deep and mysterious.

The Totem People

Totem poles and the rich traditions associated with them originated in North America among the Native peoples who made their home along this jagged coastline of the North Pacific. Totems, fascinating monuments carved usually from cedar, are unique human attempts initiated in a time long ago to

---

Ancient tales involving Raven as creator, trickster,
and transformation expert are often depicted on totem poles.

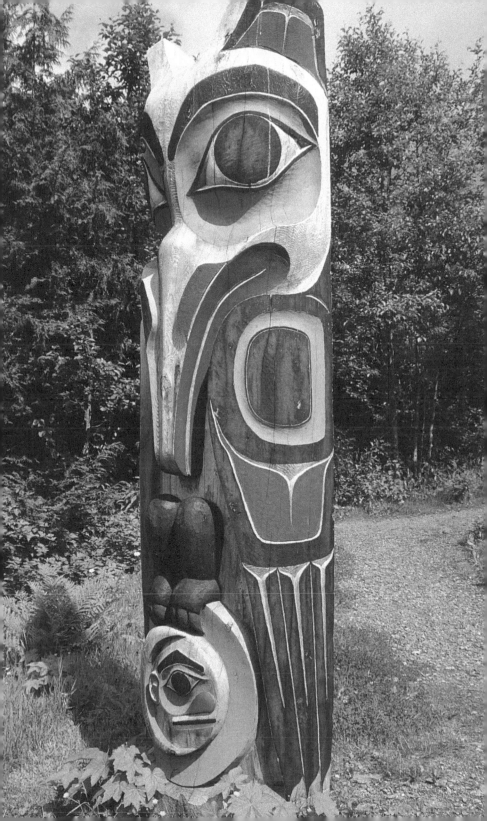

create a record of each generation's presence and passing.

From north to south, North America's Totem People are classified by the languages they speak. The Tlingit (KLIN-kit or TLIN-kit) are the Northwest Coast Indians who have lived in Alaska from ancient times. Two more recent arrivals are the Haida (HIDE-uh) and the Tsimshian (SIM-she-an) peoples. These groups share several cultural practices, including the making of totem poles.

Sharing in Alaska's totem tradition are several tribes from the province of British Columbia, Canada, and northern Washington state, extending about 900 miles as the crow flies along the western

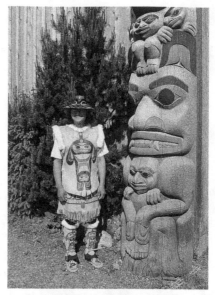

Tsimshian carver Wayne Hewson, wearing traditional garb, next to a Bear Mother totem in Metlakatla.

Pacific coastline. Occupying the same ecologic zone—the temperate rain forest—these Native tribes together make up the Totem People.

Originally, totem poles with their intricately carved figures were meant to convey important messages to passersby about the family and social status of the people who lived in a particular house in a certain village. Carved from a huge log of red or yellow cedar or sometimes Sitka spruce, a totem pole allowed related members of a family clan to portray their family rights and stories through displaying authorized crests, or symbolic emblems. Oft-depicted crest figures in Alaska included Raven, Wolf, Eagle, Bear, Whale, Frog, as well as an assortment of heroes and supernatural creatures.

Tribal members could view a totem and, by recognizing the crests, could identify the family's lineage, status, and perhaps some of its significant accomplishments if depicted. A few crests told the story of the people's migration into their present homeland, often relayed as stories of Raven leading them on a great journey. Other crests explained the family link to the spirit world of nature; for example, members of the Blackfish (or Killer Whale) clan of the Angoon Tlingit believed that one of their ancestors once visited the Blackfish underwater village and, before returning, received a magical seaweed blanket, copper canoe, and other emblems now exclusive to them.

The official claiming of crests for use on totem poles and other carvings and regalia was a solemn part of an important ceremony known as the potlatch. These crests became rallying points to which each family member pledged his or her allegiance. Despite early misunderstandings by missionaries and outsiders in general, totem poles were not worshipped.

ALASKA'S NORTHWEST COAST INDIAN TRIBES

From earliest known times, Tlingit people have resided along the Alaska Panhandle between Icy Bay in the north and the Dixon Entrance in the south. Sometime during the seventeenth century, a century or more before the Russians and Europeans began to arrive, a small group of Haida people, originally from the Queen Charlotte Islands (Haida Gwaii) in Canada, arrived on the southern half of Prince of Wales Island—hardly surprising, since the Haida were famous for their excellent Western red cedar canoes. They set up their own villages, sometimes at abandoned Tlingit sites, either though arrangement with the Tlingit or by warring conquest, and they settled and became known as the Kaigani Haida. Inevitably, Tlingit and Haida peoples occasionally interacted, intermarried, and influenced each other's cultural traditions including totem traditions, stories, and styles of carving. Today Alaska's Haida number around 300 individuals. Their reputation for excellence in totem carving far outweighs their Alaska numbers.

As for Alaska's Tsimshian, in 1887 a group of 823 people whose totem traditions originated around the Nass and Skeena rivers in British Columbia, Canada, emigrated to an officially designated reservation on Annette Island. Following the beliefs of Anglican-influenced Father William Duncan, this determined group established a "Victorian enclave in the wilderness," and left behind their totem-carving ways. This settlement's traditional totem practices lay dormant until the 1970s, when a renaissance began with the arrival of culture bearers who taught songs and dances. Carver Jack Hudson returned to Metlakatla and began teaching, and culture bearers David A. Boxley followed by his son David R. Boxley began extensive research followed by the carving of dozens of poles that continue to spread their traditions among their people. •

Totem poles come in several forms, including memorial or mortuary poles, heraldic poles, house front poles, and ridicule or shame poles. Territorial totem markers—a totem crest cut into a live tree—were most notable among the Tlingit, but all tribes used them. A memorial totem raised after an elder's death often displayed a grouping of the clan crests of a deceased person. A mortuary pole sometimes housed a coffin at the top or contained a small niche for the deceased's ashes. The heraldic totem was similar to a complex family coat of arms. Among the Haida and the Tsimshian, a house frontal pole was placed on the outside front of the house to tell the heroic stories of the owning family, and the entrance to the house was sometimes carved through the base of the pole. Ridicule poles were meant to indicate that someone had incurred an unpaid debt, and a few interesting examples still exist today. Saxman Totem Village in Ketchikan has a Tlingit ridicule pole that portrays William H. Seward, noted for his role in purchasing Alaska from the Russians. Though the locals treated him with respect and gave him gifts, he was unaware that the gifts he gave them in return were considered unequal in value by his hosts, so he appeared rude. The pole displays him with his ears and nose stained red.

The meanings of totem poles have expanded since contact with Europeans in the late 1700s. One traditional Tlingit origin story states that long ago, the Old Ones were inspired to carve totems after finding a fully carved log washed

IT ALL BEGINS WITH RAVEN

Many Tlingit stories describe how the Old Ones, led by Raven, traveled from a faraway land to the place of frozen glaciers. Ethnographer Marius Barbeau says there are more than 90 Raven stories in the Haida culture, and Raven is also the central character of many Tsimshian stories. In the stories of all Totem People, the world owed its form to Raven, a supernatural creature whose trickster character combined the attributes of spirit, transformer, fool, creator, human, bird, and genius. With his out-of-control appetites, Raven was considered the author of all nature's major phenomena—sun, moon, stars, wind, tides, animals, and cedar trees. In stories that are surprisingly similar, Raven's antics also accounted for the creation of humans and their arrival in specific regions on earth. Stories such as these provide tantalizing glimpses into Alaska Native history, hint at where the ancestors may have lived, and teach respect for the natural world. ●

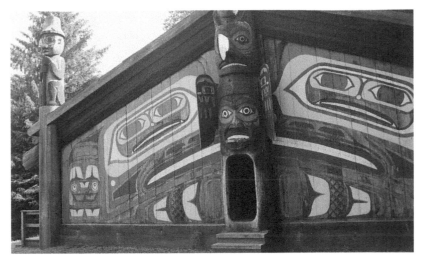

This clan house, adorned with the Raven crest, stands in Totem Bight
State Historical Park, Ketchikan. Native artists in the Civilian Conservation Corps
constructed this Native plank house in 1938.

up on a sandy beach. In another story, the Haida tell of a master carver who,
after seeing the reflection of a totem-dotted village deep within the ocean,
created a house front and several poles overnight, and then taught his fellow
villagers how to carve. Originally, totems were strictly bound up with the
kinship system of the people who made them. Original lineage-specific poles are
still being carved today, but the pole tradition has enlarged to include commem-
orations and other meanings. Today, totem crests are also used to express
Alaska's pride in all of its people, the land, its commemorative occasions, flourishing cultures, and rich traditions.

The Importance of Cedar

Totem poles evolved in this region of the world, an ecologic zone noted
for annual precipitation levels ranging from 112 to 200 inches per year. From
Southeast Alaska to the Copper River Delta, great stands of temperate rain
forest are renowned for their cathedral-like beauty. Western (or giant) red cedar
(Thuja plicata), a favored wood for carving totem poles, is widespread in
southern Alaska's coastal regions as far north as Wrangell and Petersburg. From

this area north to Hoonah and Juneau, the somewhat smaller Alaska yellow cedar (*Callitropsis nootkatensis*), which grows in boggy, rocky areas to altitudes of about 13,000 feet, is the dominant species and is used by northern totem carvers. Possibly related to the relative scarcity of cedar, you seldom see exterior totem poles north of Sitka, except for an occasional mortuary pole. For their interior house posts, such as the famous Whale house posts in Klukwan, the choice was Sitka spruce (*Picea sitchensis*). Since Alaska's coastal northern forests lack the desirable red cedar, the locals sometimes traded with southern tribes to acquire giant red cedar logs. And from time to time large red cedar logs could be found adrift in the ocean well north of their usual range.

Western red cedar wood has a soft, satin luster and can range in color from reddish cinnamon to rich sienna brown, while Alaska yellow cedar ranges from mellow amber to golden yellow. Oil in cedar gives off a distinct aroma, making cedar wood unappealing to insects, moths, and other pests, and making it resistant to decay. Growing up to 200 feet tall, well-established red cedar trees can live for perhaps 800 to 1,000 years, while yellow cedar trees may reach 500 years in age. Growing in mixed forests with other conifer

---

This drawing by Fernando Brambila of a Grizzly Mortuary Pole at Yakutat is a copy of a drawing by José Cardero, who was a ship artist with the Malaspina expedition of 1793.

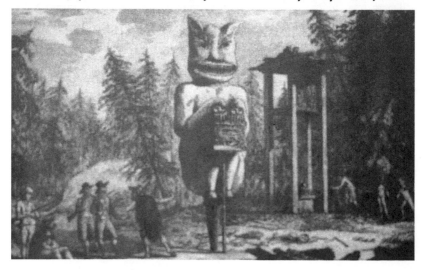

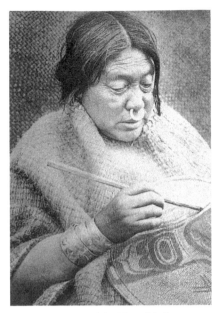

This photograph by Edward S. Curtis (ca. 1915) shows the importance of woven cedar items among Northwest Coast Indians.

species such as Douglas fir, western hemlock, Pacific yew, and Sitka spruce, cedar surpasses them all for its combined workability and durability. Distinguished by its straight grain, ease of splitting, uniform texture, and the absence of pitch, cedar carves as easily as cold butter and yet holds a fine edge. Its lack of resins creates a stable base for paints and stains.

Cedar's unique physical properties influenced both the practical and spiritual life of Northwest Coast Indians. The tree, a gift from Raven and respectfully referred to as an esteemed "sister," was used to construct house planks and pillars for traditional post-and-beam community lodges or clan houses. Within each clan house, six or seven sets of related parents, grandparents, and children—perhaps 30 to 50 people—lived their lives. Woodworkers also utilized cedar to make hundreds of utilitarian and ceremonial objects including ornately carved interior house posts, masks for elaborate ceremonial dances, rattles, and drum logs, steam-bent fishhooks, spears, and fish clubs, bentwood boxes for storage, and household food containers, cradles, and mortuary boxes as well as totem poles. Girls learned from their grandmothers how to skillfully shred red cedar bark strips, roll them into ropes and fish nets, or weave them into waterproof hats, capes, and skirts. Yellow cedar required soaking and boiling before it was pounded into strips, interwoven with duck down or mountain goat wool, and made into soft blankets. Skilled artisans ornamented most of these items with family crests.

Some believe that in ancient times, Northwest Coastal peoples made totemic emblems that were smaller in scale. Staffs with totem figures, which look like miniature totem poles the size of a walking cane, are on display in some museum collections. These objects may be song leader staffs or "talking sticks" carried by clan leaders, and had some of the same functions as totem poles—crest display. As Alaska's Native peoples acquired metal tools through contact with explorers, the ease and speed of carving totem poles increased. As a result of cultural and economic factors and despite periodic declining populations due to disease and fewer trained artists, village houses with nearby totems increased in size and number.

Before contact, master carvers made coloring agents from ground-up stones, earth, and salmon eggs mixed with seawater and saliva, creating hues more accurately described as stains. Traditional pigments for red and yellow were iron-stained earth ochres. Black sometimes came from bone burned down to form charcoal. Blue-green was derived from the mica mineral celandonite, also called "green earth," a form of hydrated iron potassium silicate. After contact, manufactured paints swiftly came into use. Paintbrush handles were cylindrical, of various materials including wood or bone, often with one spatulate end. Into this, porcupine guard hairs, sea otter hairs, or other fibers were inserted, bound, and trimmed at broad or sharp angles according to the artist's need.

Individuals used cottonwood dugout canoes for fishing in tide pools or moving about. But groups of warriors or hunters on long commutes paddled large oceangoing dugout red cedar canoes that seated up to 50 people. To make these huge canoes, skilled artisans, using chisels made from yew wood, antler, and stone, cut a notch into the trunk of a huge growing tree. Setting a small controlled fire, they burned the notch wider, opening the gap until the tree toppled over. Once the tree was felled, the carvers sculptured the outside of the hull, then very carefully carved away the inside, leaving the hull

NO WORD FOR ART

Though the Totem People had no formal word for "art," they embellished their lives with carved and painted symbols, even applying crests to every household item including spoons, bowls, and individual items of clothing. It was taken for granted that life was an unbroken tradition of creative expression filled with pictorial wisdom. ●

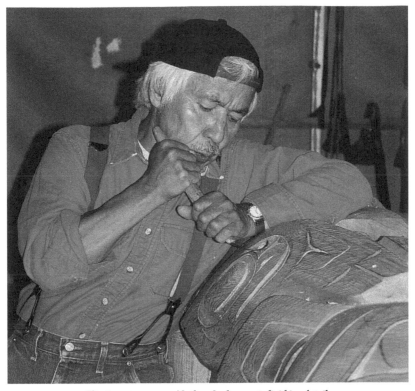

**Tlingit master carver Nathan Jackson puts finishing details
on a totem at Saxman Totem Park near Ketchikan.**

uniformly thick. To increase the size of the canoe, the strength of its sides, and its stability, the carvers filled the interior channel with water and hot stones that caused the water to boil. They steamed out the heartwood and pried the sides apart. The paddlers' cross-braced seats served to keep the boat's hull taut. The Haida manufactured transport canoes legendary for their size and speed, and the Tlingit sometimes bartered with the Haida for fully completed vessels.

The Haida prized the huge yellow cedar logs found in their territory. This wood was especially desired for digging sticks, bows, masks, dishes, paddles, and particularly distinguished totem poles. Able navigators swarmed the ocean while Native traders, especially among Tlingit-speaking tribes, guarded overland trade routes up over the Coast Range to Indian tribes of the Interior. Authorized persons were responsible for transporting boxes filled with fatty fish paste oil, alternately known as eulachon or candlefish grease, used as a condiment for dipping food or for setting alight, plus shells and other desirable coastal items. The trade routes were known as "grease trails."

Carving a Totem Pole

Cedar logs, once painstakingly felled by chisels and fire, today are swiftly brought down with chain saws. Cedar trees suitable for totem poles are found in the densest part of the forest. Here, trees compete for sunlight, branches grow solely on the upper third of the tree, and the trunks are tall and straight with few knots.

Once a felled tree trunk is safely placed inside the carving shed, the head carver assembles a team of one to five apprentices to help with the carving and holds meetings with the people who have commissioned the pole. Knowledge of exactly how to work totem crests is something that an apprentice carver learns from years at a master carver's side. Those who are diligent helpers may someday see their own names associated with carved masks and totems. After the totem's patrons have indicated which crests they prefer, the master carver either renders old crest stories for them or creates new crests using traditional guidelines. To understand a totem's meaning, it is necessary both to know what the patron wanted and how the carver interpreted those requests. In ancient times, totem pole stories and symbols were shared orally through the generations. Sometimes stories were altered or lost. So in the case of a few very old totems, figure-by-figure explanations are typically not intact today, at least in a form accessible to people outside the clans that commissioned and owned the carvings.

The average progress for a solo carver is about one foot per week, though as with any building project, times may vary. When several carvers participate, the work speeds up. The design of the totem pole is roughly drawn on a planning sheet, then it is transferred to the log itself. Modern carvers use power tools to rough out the shapes along the length of the enormous log. Traditional carvers once used adzes with handles made from yew or other hard wood, and carving tools with sharp blades made of finely grained stone, jade, or beaver teeth. Some metal blades may have been acquired prior to contact from drift

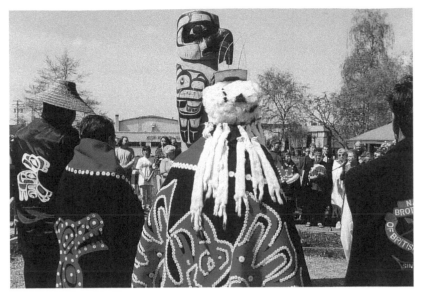

When a new Eagle totem honoring all Northwest Coast Indian tribes was raised in Vancouver, B.C., in 2000, invited guests came from as far away as Alaska and Seattle.

iron—spikes or other hardware attached to wood that drifted ashore on the Pacific tide.

On many mature cedars, the center of the trunk is rotting away. To make the final pole lighter, easier to handle, and to prevent the pole from cracking as it dries, some carvers hollow out the back into a U-shape. Others leave the trunk intact. As the bark is removed, the heady fragrance of cedar oil fills the shed. Red cedar has an incense-like fragrance while yellow cedar smells like raw potatoes.

Throughout the carving process, the totem's patrons traditionally were expected to keep the carvers warm and happy. Besides feeding them and providing occasional entertainment, small gifts are given—from a gesture as simple as a few apples or a homemade pie to something as elaborate as a potluck dinner. The head carver is responsible for supervising the apprentices, who today are usually given tasks on the upper end of the totem where mistakes are less visible.

Finally the day for the pole-raising ceremony draws near. The master carver meets with the elders of the tribe to create an approved agenda for the ceremonial raising procedures. The team moves the completed totem pole into position for the big day. And in most cases, during the evening before the pole raising there is a private gala for the carvers and the patrons.

At the climactic raising event, elders in full regalia arrive in a procession, and the master carver is honored. Various members of the tribe perform dances, sing songs, make speeches, and give blessings. In the old days, crews of workers rolled the totem into an inclined trench about 20 feet in length. Gradually filling in the trench, they maneuvered ropes and pikes to coax the totem skyward. Today, a heavy machinery operator may make quick work of raising a heavy totem pole. At the end of the ceremony, then as now, the patrons thank everyone in attendance with a small gift, ranging from an art print to a piece of fruit given in appreciation for the participants' bearing witness to and thus validating the event. A community dinner—the requisite feasting—completes the day.

Commissioning a totem is expensive. Costs today vary from $1,000 to $5,000 per foot, depending on the reputation of the carver. Traditionally, master totem carvers invoke respect, and today some are internationally recognized. A few are beloved, as much for their willingness to teach their craft as for their extraordinary design and carving skills. Totem poles represent a cultural renaissance among Indian groups who only a century ago were reputed to be a dying people. Today's master carvers work diligently to keep totem traditions alive, and to pass them on to each new generation of carvers as vibrant testimony to their flourishing culture and its revival.

THE FIRST DRAWINGS OF TOTEM POLES

John Webber, official artist for Capt. James Cook's third expedition in 1778, made a field sketch (and another artist produced an engraving from the drawing) of two Nuu-chah-nulth (formerly Nootka) house posts that he observed on what is now Canada's Vancouver Island. While simplistic, the Webber drawing is a remarkably accurate portrayal of the architecture and many of the objects. In 1791, seaman John Bartlett sketched a crude but apparently accurate ink image while traveling aboard the American trader *Gustavus.* Having viewed a scene at Dadens, a Haida village in what is now the Queen Charlotte Islands (Haida Gwaii), Bartlett made his drawing, and noted "the entrance was cut out of a large tree and carved all the way up and down." •

Early Totem Sightings

Though archaeologists claim that Pacific Northwest Coast Indians have occupied this region for at least 10,000 years, Native historians like to say that the land was granted to the Old Ones from the beginning of time.

Since oral stories vary greatly, our totem detective story starts out less poetically with a survey of the journals of the first Russian, European, and American seagoing expeditions to the shores of the entire Northwest Coast. Numerous documents indicate that when these early explorers arrived in the mid to late 1700s, totem poles were an uncommon sight. While the Alaska Indian tradition of carving crests into a variety of stone, bone, shell, and wooden objects from spoons to grave markers has roots that go back for thousands of years, post-contact spread of metal tools contributed to a flurry of major building projects, including increased construction of large clan houses and ever more ornate totem poles.

Since there was no non-Native word for "totem pole" and outsiders were unfamiliar with Native traditions, ship's log keepers devised various descriptions for their observations of carved monuments. In the decade after 1785, most expedition ship records make no note of these carvings, though one ship log documents an American captain and his crew helping to raise a totem pole.

Of France's La Pérouse party at Lituya Bay in 1786, the Tlingit were said to have responded to the strange sight of ships in this manner: "They seemed to be great black birds with immense white wings. . . ." The onboard ship's artist left engravings of the Tlingit people and their villages without totems. Visiting the Yakutat Tlingit in 1787, British Capt. George Dixon described the crests he saw on everyday objects as "figures . . . of hieroglyphics: fishes and other animals, heads of men and various whimsical designs." And British Capt. John Meares among the Haida in 1788 described both painted house fronts and "great wooden images."

Later the same year, the Nuu-chah-nulth (formerly Nootka) people of British Columbia's Vancouver Island spared the life of John R. Jewitt, the blacksmith aboard the American trading vessel *Boston*, but forced him into slavery. After three years, he escaped and later wrote of "large trees carved and painted" where he had been captive. In 1791, French naval officer and writer Charles Pierre Claret Fleurieu, documenting the voyages of French merchant Capt. Etienne Marchand who visited various islands in the Queen Charlotte group,

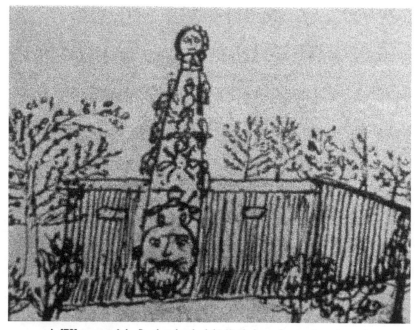

In 1791, seaman John Bartlett sketched this Haida house front pole and noted,
"The passage into the house was between the teeth."

described a Haida entrance door totem: "The head of this statue is dressed with
a cap in the form of a sugar loaf," adding pertinent information that the carvings
were "of vibrant red, black and apple green color." And the Spanish expedition
of 1792 led by Dionisio Galiano and Cayetano Valdés yielded ship artist José
Cardero's sketches of carved posts at Yakutat.

A year later, British Capt. George Vancouver described a double
mortuary column, house poles, and detached totems. On an expedition in
1791, Spanish Capt. Alejandro Malaspina, visiting the Tlingit at Lituya Bay,
recorded an upright Grizzly figure holding a mortuary box (see page 12):
"We do not know whether the colossal monster . . . is an idol or merely a
frightful record of the destructive nature of death. . . . The height of the
monster was no less than ten and a half feet." The Naval Museum in Madrid
attributes this sketch to Ferdinando Brambilla, as based on a drawing by ship
artist José Cardero.

It was in 1794 that Yankee trader Capt. H. Roberts, aboard the *Jefferson*, stopped at a Haida village on what would later be known as Dall Island, and became the first outsider to record the raising of a totem pole. "To ingratiate themselves . . . the captain with the carpenter and some of the crew went to the village to plane and smooth a wooden pole. The next day they returned with two spare top-masts and the necessary tackle to raise the pole and set it in position." At the request of Chief Cunneah, Roberts's crew painted the pole (using ship paint), placed a carved "toad" on top, and raised it. There is no word on the celebrations that no doubt followed.

A review of these early expedition logs indicates that while monumental wooden carvings were not yet the overwhelming sights they would later become, they were present in small numbers. By 1799 and later, totem poles were more common. British seafarer Capt. George Dixon aboard the *Eliza* reported Haida communal mortuary poles at Kiusta. Two journal keepers, young John Boit, aboard American Capt. Gray's *Columbia*, and Robert Haswell, aboard the *Lady Washington*, both reported house entrance poles at Clayquot. However in a later voyage, Ludovik Andreevich Choris, lithographer with Russian explorer Otto von Kotzebue's voyage between 1815 and 1817, left rich pictorial records of their more northerly coastal explorations, but no renditions of any crest figures.

Beginning in 1784 and working their way eastward, Russian traders acting under the auspices of the Shelikov-Golikov Company began an accelerated harvesting of sea otters. Quickly decimating the numbers of animals in the Aleutians, then the Kodiak region, the Southeast was their third and final stop. By the end of 1799, Tsar Paul I, son of the late Russian Empress Catherine the Great, granted sole trading rights to a new entity, the Russian-American Company, to handle territorial fur trade, with Alexander Baranov as company manager and first governor of Russian Alaska. During the operation of the Russian-American Company, 34 posts were established. The St. Michael trading post operated near present-day Sitka. Staffed with Russian labor and enslaved Aleut people, the frenetic harvesting operation of sea otter furs continued.

In June 1802, enraged Tlingit destroyed the fort, killing many. A British sea captain, Henry Barber, rescued some survivors, took them to Kodiak, and was paid 10,000 rubles in furs by Baranov to cover his expenses. Two years later, Baranov rebuilt a new settlement, naming it New Archangel and declaring it the capital of Russian America. It would later be renamed Sitka. In 1804, Baranov, aided with cannon fire from Russian Capt.-Lt. Urey Fedorovich Lisianski's ship *Neva*, retaliated against the Tlingit and many lives were lost. Lisianski was a commanding officer in the Imperial Russian Navy in the process of attempting a Russian circumnavigation of the world. Of the mortuary boxes he observed after this battle, Lisianski wrote, "The bodies here are burned, and the ashes, together with the bones that remain unconsumed, deposited in wooden boxes which are placed on pillars that have different figures painted and carved on them, according to the wealth of the deceased. On taking possession of our new settlement we destroyed a hundred at least of these, and I examined many of the boxes . . . the colors were black, light green and dark red." Of monumental wooden carvings he wrote: "These families, however, always live apart; and, to distinguish the caste to which they belong, they place on the top of their houses, carved in wood or painted, the bird or beast that represents it."

The Golden Age of Totem Poles

Almost as soon as Russia dominated Alaska's fur trade, America's "Boston Men" and Britain's Hudson's Bay Company traders stubbornly made inroads into the Russian monopoly. Sensing a profit to be made, in 1834 nine Tsimshian villages set up trading outposts just south of Alaska, outside Fort Simpson in British Columbia. Older village leaders appointed younger relatives to manage the new outposts. This turn of events resulted in a series of rivalry potlatches. Dozens of new totems were carved to sort out the newly elevated status of the outpost leaders.

Throughout Southeast Alaska, some Natives moved closer to communities where work was available, and common people became richer than the elders they left behind. Whereas traditionally, only a few people could afford to commission a totem, from 1830 to 1880 hundreds of newly rich working people indulged in one of these big-ticket items for their village. Historic photographs of coastal Alaska villages during the late 1880s and 1890s, sometimes called totems' Golden Age, show "forests of totem poles," especially in the southern half of southeast Alaska where red cedar was more readily available.

But as epidemics ravaged the population over and over again, leadership crumbled, survivors became demoralized, and the unique and complex family system of the Northwest Coast Indians that included totem crests began to break down. Without slave labor, the upper and middle classes who occupied traditional clan houses found that no one was willing to cut and carry wood. Villagers, more or less abandoning their Native-style homes, moved into American-style bungalows on the outskirts of growing towns. Some of the old villages, recently revitalized with new totem poles and clan houses, began to empty. In the deserted villages, the rain forest encroached on doorways, weather eroded abandoned longhouses, and vines grew around untended totem poles.

By about 1860, for various reasons including the near extinction of sea otters, Russian interest in its Alaska territory had declined. In 1867, U.S.

A COLLECTING FRENZY

During the late 1700s and the 1800s, dozens of research voyages to Alaska were funded by various nations. "Science" was the buzzword of the day and scientific expeditions were very popular with the public. One example was an expedition supported by Russia's Academy of Sciences in 1839, in which scientist I. G. Voznesenskii was sent to study the region's Native populations. After a 10-year visit he brought back thousands of artifacts. Among the prominent researchers of the day, Captain J. A. Jacobsen, ethnographer for the Berlin Museum, when returning from an 1883 expedition, boasted that he had personally acquired more than 6,000 objects, many of them Tlingit. Over the next century, travelers from sailors to religious clerics collected masks and carvings, helmets and clubs, rattles and fishhooks, bowls and boxes, blankets and combs. For a period of 40 years before and after the turn of the twentieth century, academics raced each other to build collections. Museum displays popularized three basic concepts: wild plants, wild animals, and "primitive" people.

Wealthy patrons collected artifacts, spurred on by the myth of a vanishing race. For example, J. L. Kraft, founder of Kraft Foods, collected Northwest Coast totem poles, one of which was long displayed on Chicago's lakefront.

As a result of this activity, early Alaskan Indian art pieces are displayed in major museums throughout the world, ranging from the Museum of Fine Arts in St. Petersburg, Russia, to the Menil Collection in Houston, Texas. ➤

Since 1990, with the implementation of the Native American Graves

Secretary of State William Seward negotiated the purchase of Alaska from Russia for $7.2 million. Critics attacked the purchase as "Seward's Folly." The *New York Tribune* coined the term "Walrussia" for what was represented as a worthless, frozen wasteland. Historic as the transaction is portrayed, Native claims were not considered in the process. It took until 1924 for Congress to extend official citizenship to Native Americans.

Devastating Changes

The inroads that Christianity made among Native Alaskans was accelerated by the more than a century of periodic epidemics. As early as 1791, French surgeon Claude Roblet with the Marchand expedition, like Capt. Dixon before him, recorded signs of smallpox around the Sitka area. Throughout the 1800s, there may have been as many as six major epidemics of various diseases, some occurring simultaneously, others occurring a few decades apart. But the final

A COLLECTING FRENZY continued

Protection and Repatriation Act (NAGPRA), Indian tribes have begun to exercise newly defined rights to Native American human remains, funerary objects, sacred objects, and cultural objects. The Act requires federal agencies and museums to provide information about Native American cultural items to parties with standing, and upon presentation of a valid request, dispose of or repatriate these objects to them. Subsequently many tribes throughout North America are either in active negotiation or prolonged court procedures to reclaim many of their former items. Notable among these were the takings from the 1899 Harriman Expedition (see page 27).

In July 2001, Seattle's Burke Museum along with the Peabody Essex Museum, the Field Museum, the National Museum of the American Indian, and Cornell University's Johnson Museum of Art repatriated house posts, a totem pole, and hundreds of cultural objects to descendants of the Cape Fox Tlingit tribe near Ketchikan. And in 2003, the Tlingit people in Angoon repatriated a Bear totem, the symbol of their Teikweidi or Bear clan. Disappearing about 1908, it had been located in six different locations on the Greeley campus of the University of Northern Colorado, where it inspired their sports team mascot "Totem Teddy." •

blow to the old ways began in 1900 with the arrival of the "Great Death." Reeling from the effects of smallpox, measles, diphtheria, and pneumonia, Alaska's Indians experienced waves of polio and tuberculosis. Famine accompanied the deadly march of disease. In a period of 20 years, up to two-thirds of Alaska's Natives lost their lives.

Throughout these devastating periods, American missionaries tended to the sick and built orphanages. As a routine part of their ministering duties, Christian workers discouraged traditional practices as they sincerely tried to improve the Natives' lives. It was but a few religious leaders who were forward thinking as well as charitable. For example, in 1882 Presbyterian missionaries John G. Brady (later territorial governor of Alaska) and Fannie Kellogg opened an old Sitka military barracks as a Tlingit training school. Though the original building burned to the ground, Rev. Sheldon Jackson organized a nationwide fund-raising campaign, and Sheldon Jackson College had its beginning in 1878. Shortly afterward, the Tlingit asked Jackson to establish a Tlingit mission near Haines.

As Presbyterian superintendent of the Home Missions of the Territories and later as First General Agent of Education in Alaska, Jackson worried that Native cultures would disappear. To this end, throughout his journeys he collected thousands of items including totem poles and placed them in educational displays. To house his collections in Sitka, construction began in 1895 on a museum that has been in use since 1897. One of Jackson's goals in establishing the museum was to help future generations of Alaska Natives learn how their forebears lived. Both vocational programs and a museum at Sitka were to bear his name. In 2007, Sheldon Jackson College suspended operation, but the Sheldon Jackson Museum persists.

Most government educators and Christian missionaries, however, believed that totem poles were part of the old ways that needed to be enthusiastically discouraged. Though some missionaries held carving classes to produce artwork or souvenir curios in their schools as vocational training, they felt that the original belief system represented in the totem carvings competed with their efforts to Christianize and civilize the Natives. They demanded that Natives cease carving the poles and in some cases burn them. Totem-making in Alaska virtually ceased by 1901, and the practices that went with the tradition slowly began to fade away.

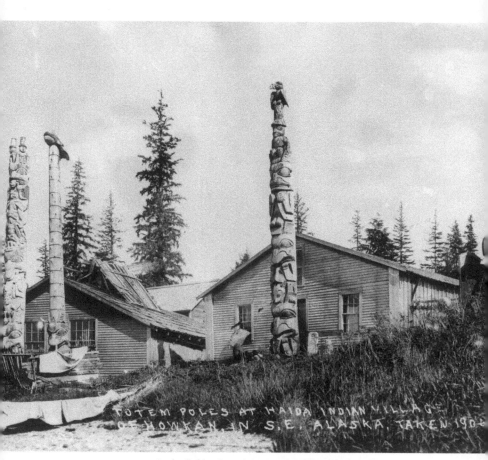

TOTEM POLES AT HAIDA INDIAN VILLAGE OF HOWKAN, IN S.E. ALASKA. TAKEN 1904

In the Golden Age of totem poles, villages such as
Howkan were studded with totems.

Symbol of the Pacific Northwest

Set against this recurring devastation, and adapting to a glut of fur
traders, government agents, and missionaries, by 1885, Alaska's Natives
encountered a new group of outsiders. Pampered travelers began arriving
from Seattle by steamship. These early tourists explored "the Last Frontier,"
marveled at Alaska's glaciers, and traveled ashore to purchase curios. Native
artists shrewdly took the opportunity to produce souvenir totems. Next,

prospectors and storekeepers began to arrive by the thousands. And scientific exploration also continued apace. Financed by railroad magnate Edward H. Harriman in 1899, a distinguished group of 126 famous and influential scientists, naturalists, artists, and writers assembled a "floating university" to study the new land. In the spirit of the times, they collected thousands of items including a few totem poles. Official photographers for the Harriman Expedition included the famed Edward S. Curtis, who took striking photos of villages complete with toppling poles. These pictures proved especially popular with the news media of the day, adding to the popularity of this unique Indian art form—totem poles.

In addition to academics and tourists, several well-attended international expositions made the concept of "totem poles" a household term. The 1876 Centennial Exposition in Philadelphia and the 1893 World's Columbia Exposition in Chicago both displayed a few traditional totem poles from Alaska along with a mixed assortment of other artifacts from Native peoples. A guidebook stated, "It is more than probable that the World's Columbia Exposition will furnish the last opportunity for an acquaintance with the 'noble red-man' before he achieves annihilation." For even as totems were rotting away in Alaska's Native villages, crowds of faraway strangers were identifying the totem pole as the new symbol of the Pacific Northwest Coast.

The first large-scale effort by the U.S. government to preserve totem poles came when the governor of the District of Alaska, John Brady, collected about two dozen poles in Alaska for display at expositions in St. Louis and Portland in 1904 and 1905. Creation of artworks and ceremonies continued to take place throughout the twentieth century, in spite of efforts to suppress them. Ceremonies were driven underground and the art was different from before and not as visible, but traditions persisted. In Canada, the potlatch was outlawed until the 1950s, and in Alaska, there was the widespread assumption that it was either against the law or it was frowned upon by powerful people. While the totem tradition never faded away completely, it wasn't until the government organized large-scale totem restoration efforts in the 1930s, and dedicated enthusiasts researched and revived the old ways in the 1960s and 1970s, that Pacific Northwest Coast totem art and its related ceremonies experienced a full and rich renaissance. ∎

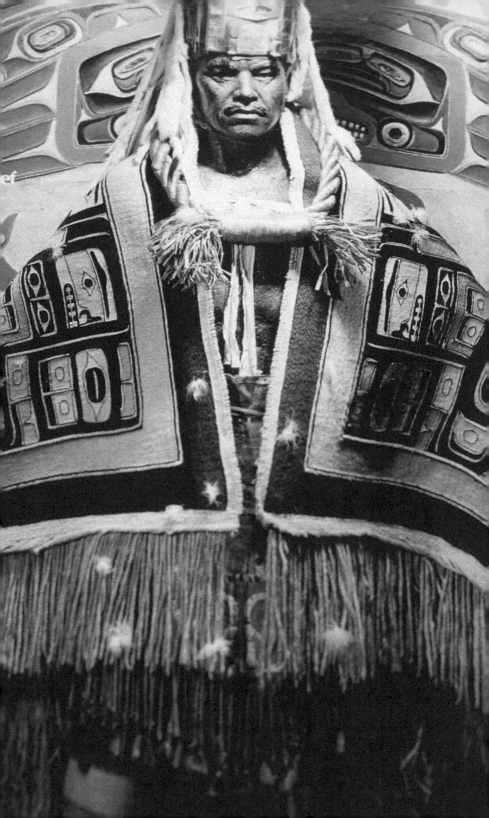

CHAPTER 2

Totem Traditions

The meanings and traditions surrounding totem poles have steadily evolved over the past two centuries. While old totems were a series of authorized crests and story figures relating to clan history or serving as memorials to deceased leaders, they also enhanced the status of the owners, and in rare cases advertised debts owed by other groups. Today the focus of totem poles is broader. Skillful Native master carvers improvise new crests based on traditional forms to immortalize their village founders, celebrate an historic state occasion, a scientific discovery, or cooperation between groups.

Pacific Northwest Coast Indian Society

To understand the traditional meaning of totems, ethnographers have spent more than 150 years sorting out how indigenous Alaskans once organized their social structure. At the time of contact, the Tlingit, Haida, and Tsimshian peoples operated in a kinship system that included three levels: an

---

A museum diorama depicts a Tsimshian chief wearing a Chilkat blanket
and a woven cedar collar, a symbol of his authority.

upper ruling class, a middle level of commoners, and slaves. Highest in rank were the chiefs, subchiefs, and elders responsible for the bureaucratic leadership of their households and villages. Although their power was limited, skilled members of wealthy aristocratic families who proved worthy of the position tended to occupy the domain of clan leadership. Advised by shamans, they administrated day-to-day living, marriages, adoptions, potlatches, inheritance rights, hunting expeditions, and building projects. To avenge wrongs, they initiated and led war parties, kidnapped slaves, plundered booty, and had transgressors punished. At ceremonies and potlatches, they wore distinctive ceremonial dress, performed special dances, told exclusive stories, raised totem poles, bestowed thousands of gifts, and displayed shield-shaped objects called "coppers," a symbol of prestige. Elders at this level enjoyed the warmest place by the fire, the first choice of fresh game, and the finest crafted objects, which when not in use they might store behind the large decorated screens at the back of their houses. They had rights to the best fishing places on the river and the most productive hunting areas in the forest. Furthermore, their relatives monopolized the best trade routes and their women held exclusive picking rights to the best berry patches.

Next in line was a class of commoners, which included most of the skilled labor force such as artisans, traders, hunters and fishers, and other ordinary folks. Common villagers could be elevated to the upper ranks through marriage or adoption. The primary way of raising status among men was by being a useful person who was viewed as an excellent tribal citizen, followed the culture, excelled in his work, and gained wealth through that success. Valuable activities ranged from serving as members of hunting parties or military forays, manufacturing hunting or fishing implements and bentwood boxes, or carving masks, canoes, and totem poles.

Women passed on their family names to their children and enjoyed the rights associated with the husband they married. Upper-class women led a life of relative leisure, whereas middle-class women could expect to earn commodities primarily from creating ceremonial costume pieces; spinning, dyeing, and weaving blankets; or making waterproof cedar-bark clothing. Assigned in the late nineteenth century, at least in name, to the Chilkat people of the villages of Klukwan and the Chilkat River Valley, the knowledge to

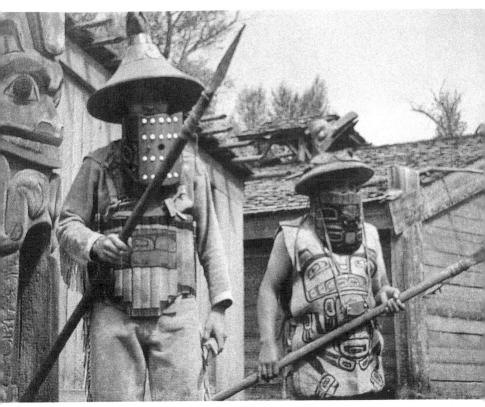

Tsimshian warriors wear traditional slatted wooden armor in reenactments of plundering raids or of defending their villages.

design and weave crest-laden Chilkat blankets, which may have originated elsewhere, ultimately spread among many tribes.

Except for ceremonial occasions, there were no set mealtimes. Long strips of salmon and game, dried into a kind of "jerky" in a smokehouse, was sometimes hung from the rafters of the house to protect the food supply from marauding bears. Family members helped themselves during the fishing season. Dried food was then packed away in bentwood boxes, and served from bentwood serving containers. At low tide, people walked out to the abundant oyster, mussel, and clam beds. Women were expected to keep supplies of dried berries, boiled salmon, deer, or cooked seal meat handy in a place near the fire. The entire population, including leaders, commoners, and slaves, fathers, mothers, and even the children worked together in an organized way to amass enough food to make it through the lean time of year. Gathering food and preparing it to prevent spoilage was a huge undertaking; their survival depended on their success.

At the bottom of the social scale were slaves captured in war raids or born to other slaves. Treated as property with no personal freedom, they performed menial work like serving others and keeping the fires lit. Slaves were traded or freed as their owners wished. For elite families, slaves provided them with an important source of labor for producing surplus goods both for trade and gift giving. As for the daily life of the slaves, American George T. Emmons (1852–1945), ethnographic photographer and navy lieutenant, reported that among the Tlingit, it "depended entirely upon the character of the master," and that usually "their condition of life differed little from that of the poorer class. They hunted, fished, handled the canoe, and did all kinds of manual labor, as did all others, and in turn were fed, clothed, and housed."

TALKING STICKS

Prominent on two totems flanking the clan house at Totem Bight State Historical Park, "talking sticks" or "speaker's staffs" once were a badge of office for a leader. Some of the staffs, especially among the Tlingit, were used by song leaders during singing and dancing. Some historians believe that these sticks were the precursors to totem poles. ●

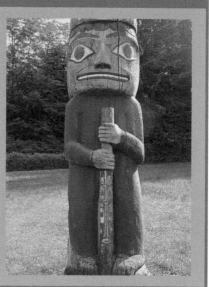

An elder holds a talking stick, a policy-making symbol.

To show one's rank and identity within this class system, people embellished their personal objects with a selection of crests owned communally through their family lineage. Authorized symbols were present on house fronts, interior and exterior walls, war canoes, weapons, storage boxes, eating utensils, ceremonial masks and costumes, apparel, personal blankets, shirts, footwear, jewelry, and of course, totem poles. Some Haida and Tlingit even tattooed their clan crests on their arms, legs, chests, and backs. Displaying a new crest on household items and regalia, for example, identified the changing social position of a family or family member.

Besides a relationship to one's mother, father, uncles, aunts, cousins, and so on, each person was classified within a kinship system comparable to a corporate management structure. According to varying systems of complexity within each of the tribes, the largest family divisions, called moieties or phratries, were first subdivided into clans or local lineages, then subdivided again into smaller units called houses. Each division was identified with a series of authorized crests, rights, wonders, and privileges. "Owning" crests meant that a moiety, clan, or house had rights to display authorized emblems. And sometimes those emblems signaled specific territorial rights—such as owning the best fishing areas—exercised exclusively by them. In some cases, "wonders" were claims to favors from supernatural spirits, and "privileges" were daily benefits such as being served first, second, or third in what we might today call protocol.

Southeast Alaska's Native kinship system was matrilineal. Each person's clan membership, name, and status were passed down at birth from one's mother. Tribal grandmothers played a special role in ceremonial occasions, and all-important privileges, rights, and prerogatives were passed down through one's mother, mother's brothers (maternal uncles), and maternal grandmother. It also was important for a woman to be married to a man from a family of equal social position.

Children's names and entitlements were tracked from birth, and individuals were always on the lookout for ways to do good works. Acts of heroism could result in a boost to one's hereditary standing. Since lineage was so influential, it was forbidden for a clan or house to use another's names, rights, or crests, and major disagreements resulted if this occurred, some continuing

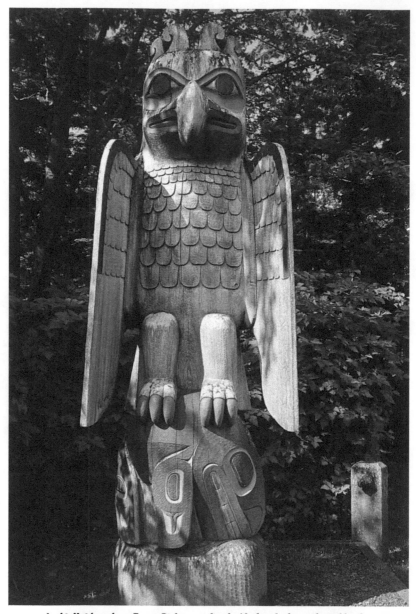

In this Haida pole at Totem Bight, a replica by Nathan Jackson of an old pole,
a stately Eagle stands over Killer Whale, also known as Blackfish.

for centuries. Fortunate indeed were those who earned additional rights through formal adoption into a new clan, lineage, or house.

Older family members arranged marriages, but the complications of choosing a spouse were many. While early ethnographers and anthropologists wrote endless academic papers on the specific details, a simple explanation is that the Tlingit classified their two moieties either as Raven and Eagle, or Raven and Wolf, while the Haida assigned their moieties as Raven and Eagle. The Tsimshian identified four divisions: Raven, Eagle, Wolf, and Killer Whale. When choosing a marriage partner, choices were limited to persons from the opposite moiety followed by several other taboos and restrictions. For example, an Eagle could only marry a Raven, and vice versa, giving rise to the concept of the Eagle and the Raven being known in totem lore as "lovebirds." Even among the Tsimshian, there were two marriage groups: The Raven and Killer Whale clans chose from the Wolf and Eagle clans, and vice versa. Elders were brought in to resolve who-was-allowed-to-marry-whom conflicts. Sometimes, if elders liked a couple, they found loopholes. Marriage was a serious commitment, though a form of divorce was common. During his lifetime, a Tlingit man averaged two wives, sometimes three. Having more wives was very expensive, so it was only done by the wealthiest men and their clans. Titled widows received a designated living allowance and were generally the responsibility of their husband's brothers.

The Traditional Potlatch

Within this complex social system, keeping track of one's status and legal rights was a must. Since these cultures had not developed a written language, it fell to the potlatch ceremony to serve as the official means to validate rights and status. Lasting for up to three weeks, the potlatch celebration distributed bounty, formalized shifting loyalties, and legalized an individual's and a family's claims to names, crests, and privileges.

Starting with several days of speeches and the parading of crests, there was a long redressing of transgressions and crimes—issues ranging from using resources from another's domain to accidental manslaughter—followed by the claiming and displaying of new privileges. Potlatch ceremonies were also accompanied by a series of feasts, a process for empowering witnesses who could later attest to the transactions, and gift giving by the hosts to the guests. For the climax, a totem pole was usually raised to formalize the granting of new crests, followed by solemn late-night secret ceremonies and masked dances.

Traditionally, Tlingit ceremonies included the memorializing of those who had passed. They hosted a potlatch for elite funerals, piercing noble children's ears, or when a new heir replaced the mother's brother. However, the Tlingit potlatch (more accurately called the memorial feast) primarily marked the end of grieving for a deceased member of the host clan and the repayment to the opposite moiety for the services they rendered during the funeral events. Other activities, such as raising poles, displaying or bringing out new crests, or the installation of a new house master, were events that could also happen during the memorial feast.

The Haida might mount a potlatch for the same reasons as the Tlingit, or for such occasions as declaring the nobility of a new child, the raising of a new house or totem pole, installing a new chief, or the ending of a clan's mourning for a deceased person. The Tsimshian potlatch could cover many of the same issues, and perhaps also commemorate the announcement of a significant social event, the birth, marriage, or death of a person of high rank, or his inheritance and ascension to a title, such as the naming of a new chief.

Today's potlatches differ from those of the past, in terms of length (now usually one or two days total) or purpose, including reaffirming heritage or honoring individuals. Gift giving is a major feature of the potlatch. Before contact, potlatch gifts might include rattles, furs, jewelry, robes, headpieces, bentwood boxes, and handwoven blankets for the upper class, with berries and fish grease for ordinary folks. After contact, gifts modernized to sewing machines, washbasins, baby clothes, hard tack, flour, sugar, traps, guns, canoes, crockery, dishes, beds, mattresses, and the ever-popular blankets. Anyone who accepted a gift was expected to bear witness to the honors being granted and to support changes in the social fabric. Gifts given at the potlatch closed out a standing debt between clans, and a reciprocal potlatch was not needed. However, if the value of gifts given at the potlatch was not in keeping with a clan or house's ranking, its status could suffer.

The potlatch was not outlawed in Alaska, though for many years American government and church officials discouraged all Native cultural practices. If our modern American system kept track of legalities through a system similar to the potlatch, and if the potlatching were then outlawed, as it was in Canada in 1884, many institutions would be unable to function. It would mean the cessation of records of land or property ownership, old age or widow's pensions, insurance payouts, health benefits, debts paid, hunting and fishing licenses, honors or medals bestowed, military service, records of births, marriages, divorces, and deaths. The ensuing chaos would be hard to

A COMPLEX SOCIETY BASED ON SALMON RUNS

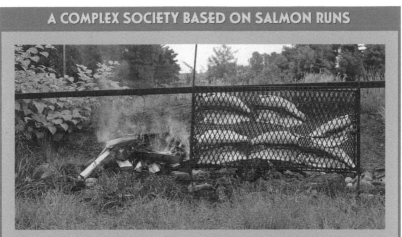

Freshly caught salmon are smoked over a pungent alder wood fire in the traditional manner.

Among the world's original societies, complicated social class divisions and kinship systems usually developed among agricultural people, such as the ancient Egyptians, rather than among hunter-gatherers. So early academics were surprised when they encountered a multilevel class and rights system well instituted among the first peoples of the Pacific Northwest and Alaska. Scholars believe that it was the assured annual gathering of thousands of salmon, the ever-abundant tidal pools, the proliferation of berry patches, and therefore the assured food supply, that acted like a regular agricultural harvest. There is a Tlingit saying, "When the tide is out, the table is set." Once a food supply is assured, people have the leisure time to develop and establish complicated social and ceremonial systems. The Indians of the Northwest Coast also benefited from a relatively moderate climate, making their life free from extreme hardship. •

fathom, though this is similar to what happened to Alaska's and Canada's Natives when the potlatch was discouraged.

When totem pole carving and the giving of traditional potlatches diminished in Alaska around 1900 and what was called "the last great traditional Tlingit potlatch" was held in 1904, a long barren period took hold in which Southeast Alaska's traditional Indian ceremonial practices nearly ceased. Natives who were members of certain Christian churches substituted surrogate observances for some traditional ceremonial functions, with potlatch traditions continuing more quietly and with some modifications.

POTLATCH WITNESSES

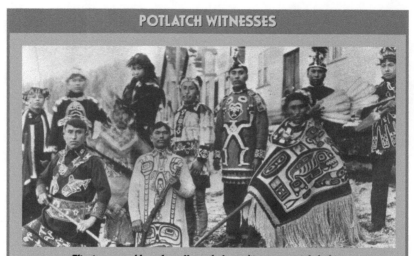

Tlingit men and boys from Hoonah dressed in ceremonial clothing to pose around a miniature cannon in this 1912 photo.

During the potlatch ceremony, members of guest clans were considered "witnesses" to the proceedings and were instructed to attentively watch while a person received his or her new honors. After the ceremony, all witnesses were rewarded with one or more gifts. The leaders of the guest clans at potlatches were generally treated better than the other guests, and given more expensive gifts in keeping with their higher status. If the honored person's new rights were ever questioned, the witnesses were expected to come at their own expense and give testimony as to what they had seen during the potlatch. Without written records, "witnessing" was the accepted way to keep track of significant events. ●

Although clans still owned crests and names, held use rights to land and property, and crimes were still punished, because of the central role of the potlatch for a considerable period the people were without an important means of transmitting and enforcing laws, status, order, good government, and wisdom. The epicenter of their social order was disrupted.

Saving Old Totems

During the first third of the twentieth century, totem carving was generally defunct in Alaska. Fortunately, a few far-seeing individuals carried out sporadic efforts to preserve the poles that remained. Alaska's District Governor John G. Brady assembled a sizable collection of Tlingit and Haida totems, first displaying them at the 1904 Louisiana Purchase Centennial Exposition in St. Louis, Missouri, then transporting them to the 1905 Lewis and Clark Centennial Exposition in Portland, Oregon. The Alaska displays at these fairs, with their lofty totem poles and two Native houses, attracted enthusiastic crowds. The well-traveled totems were eventually repatriated to the town of Sitka, first reserved in a public park by President Harrison in 1890, and then in the park designated as Sitka National Monument in 1910. At Seattle's energetic Alaska-Yukon-Pacific Exposition in 1909, four totem poles were displayed in the amusement park area of the fair, and there was at least one pole in the Alaska Building.

On the other hand, in 1913, clans from the Tlingit village of Kake destroyed all their totem poles at the forceful urging of a local minister. Twenty-four historical photographs of that village taken about the year 1900 were all that remained in a library archive. Today, those photographs are on display at the Kake Tribal Corporation Offices, though it took almost 70 years for the photos to inspire the building of new totems.

By Presidential Proclamation in 1916, Old Kasaan, a Haida enclave on Prince of Wales Island, was declared a National Monument. And by 1920, Judge James Wickersham, a man with a great appreciation for Alaska, started a movement to preserve the remaining totems at Port Tongass. Unfortunately, during a 1923 presidential visit to Alaska, Wickersham failed to have President Harding's itinerary revised. Subsequently, the Lincoln Totem Pole, a unique totem Wickersham had hoped to obtain funds to preserve, continued to decay for another 16 years.

In 1926, Dr. H. W. Kreiger of the U.S. National Museum inspected houses and totems at Old Kasaan. Though many were beyond repair, he ordered the remaining ones preserved with creosote. At about the same time, through the efforts of Gen. James Gordon Steese, president of the Alaska Road Commission, a few old poles at Sitka were repainted and raised. At Wrangell, Walter Waters experimented with preserving totems by boring holes on top and pouring rock salt into the bores. And trader Ernest Kirberger, who resided at Kake for 45 years, displayed several Tlingit totems in his store until it burned down in 1926. From 1921 to 1934, forester Charles Florey generated masses of paper lamenting the deterioration of Alaska's Native sites, while government officials systematically ignored him.

Totem Renaissance

In 1931, a group of artists, writers, and a few federal government officials decided that Native American handicrafts might enhance self-sufficiency for a poverty-stricken people. Borrowing archival pieces from museums across the United States, patron Amelia Elizabeth White and artist John Sloan privately funded an Exposition of Indian Arts in New York. Prominent art critics were invited to critique and thus legitimize Native American art.

The idea spread, and in 1934, as part of Roosevelt's New Deal, the Indian Arts and Crafts Board (IACB) was formed with the intention of encouraging the public to buy Native American artwork. In 1938, impressed with the U.S. Indian School at Ketchikan, the Sheldon Jackson School at Sitka, and souvenir totem poles, the IACB arranged a visit for board manager Rene d'Harnoncourt. His Alaska tour culminated in two well-received exhibitions in San Francisco and New York, each arranged around a dramatically illuminated 50-foot totem pole. The invited feature celebrities were Haida elder John Wallace, who had apprenticed to his carver father, plus his son, Fred. They performed dances for audiences and carved additional poles, two of which stand today at New York's Museum of Modern Art.

Throughout the 1930s and 1940s, magazine writers, interior decorators, fashion designers, and jewelry makers were actively encouraged to prod the public into emulating the style and colors favored by American

Indian peoples. The so-called "Lodge Look" emerged, complete with rustic Indian-made accessories to recall the feeling of summer camp spent by a lake or winters at a mountain retreat. Cherokee, Ojibwa, and Seminole carvers began to carve souvenir totem poles despite the fact that the totem tradition was unprecedented among their peoples. These efforts produced a jumble of perceptions about Indians in the public's mind. Teepees and totem poles mixed with feather headdresses, buffalo robes, peace pipes, and Southwest pottery. As the lore of totems mixed with these new "pop" icons, totem poles became a symbol not just for Alaska but for all North American Original Peoples.

In April 1933, President Roosevelt approved formation of the Indian Civilian Conservation Corps (CCC) to improve reservation lands. Since the

Replicating old poles started in approximately the 1930s when people became concerned about preserving fallen, decaying originals.

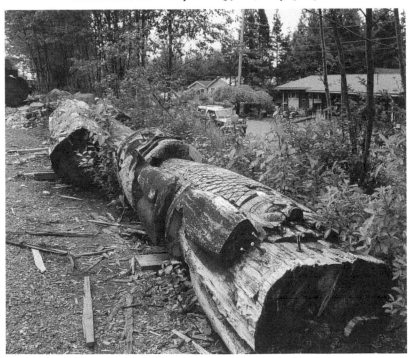

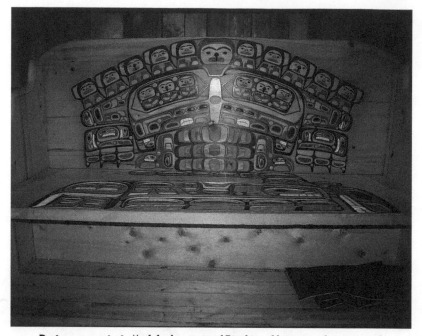

During ceremonies in Metlakatla, esteemed Tsimshian elders in regalia are seated on this bench, by Rick Booth (Tsimshian), emblazoned with community crests.

totems in Alaska were not on reservations, the funding came from the national CCC and the Works Progress Administration (WPA). By 1938, in Alaska, forester B. Frank Heintzleman, director of the CCC, was collecting forgotten totems. Of all that remained standing, about 200 were harvested. Linn A. Forrest, a well-known national lodge architect, helped resurrect old clan house designs. Eventually CCC funds of about $200,000 were gathered and nearly 250 Native carvers began to replicate old totem poles and a few clan houses. With the economic depression in full swing, people searched out nearly eroded totem poles for copying, and rediscovered how to make adzes and other handmade carving tools. After initially confusing traditional colors, samples of the original paints were analyzed and modern paints were mixed. While woodworking and painting skills were emphasized, supervisors did little to research the apprentice system, the dances, songs, or ceremonies that were also vital to the tradition.

Eventually, teams of CCC workers did replicate several ancient poles on the verge of being lost forever, and several more poles were re-carved from memory. "At least 150 of the old poles have been restored or copied, and new ones have been designed," wrote anthropologist Viola Garfield in 1944. Fragments of old poles had been laid beside freshly cut cedar logs, and good-hearted attempts made to replicate them. According to forester Harry Spalding, "The poles are being restored with faithful historical accuracy. . . . " Others disagreed. After traveling to many Pacific Northwest and Alaska totem sites beginning in 1946, Edward Malin, anthropologist, teacher of native folklore, and consultant with the U.S. Department of the Interior, argued that "the results . . . are an affront to the past." Nonetheless, totem poles that might have rotted away at that time are instead available for modern viewers to enjoy. Today the results of the CCC intervention are displayed (and in turn, once again deteriorating in the elements) in popular totem parks in Ketchikan at Saxman and Totem Bight, Sitka National Historic Park, Wrangell, Hydaburg, Kasaan, and Klawock.

The Potlatch Tradition Revives

Quietly in Haines, beginning in 1947, German immigrant Carl Heinmiller formed a friendship with Mildred Sparks, a respected Tlingit tribal elder. Using a local Boy Scout troop for practice, Heinmiller and several other enthusiasts began to resurrect the dances of the local Tlingit people. And there, in August 1952, though the dancers' masks, headdresses, and other regalia were in need of repair, the public enthusiastically witnessed once again an authentic Tlingit ceremonial dance. This event, repeated throughout Southeast Alaska over the next few decades, culminated in the founding of Alaska Indian Arts, Inc., a program of wood carving and regalia making, the construction of an authentic tribal house, and the 1957 founding of the renowned Chilkat Dancers in Haines.

Combining the ideas of Native and non-Native enthusiasts alike, towns like Haines set the stage not only for reviving totem carving but for resurrecting the old songs, dances, and ceremonies that go with the potlatch tradition. Established in 1969 and building on George Federoff's training program at Mount Edgecumbe School in Sitka in the 1960s, the Southeast Alaska Indian Cultural Center (SEAICC) today imparts local Tlingit cultural values to students and visitors. Throughout the 1960s and 1970s, serious individual carvers were slowly emerging. They set out to revive traditional ways. Many traveled to the location of their family totems, and researched museum collections; some collaborated with each other, while others worked on their own. They practiced their skills, verified their traditions, and began to teach others the ancient styles of Pacific Northwest Coast art. One old master carver, Mungo Martin, a Kwakiutl artist who had carved in secret for many years, set up an open workshop behind the Provincial Museum in Victoria, B.C., in 1952. There he inspired dozens of apprentices from throughout British Columbia and Alaska. Next emerged two influential contributors to the elevation of totem artistry and design, art historian Bill Holm in Seattle and Haida master carver Bill Reid in Vancouver, B.C.

At the 1964 World's Fair in New York, the igloo-shaped Alaska Pavilion was fronted with the three well-traveled 30-foot totems originally exhibited at the 1904 St. Louis World's Fair. By 1969, Alaska Indian Arts, Inc., in Haines had produced the world's largest totem pole to date via the work of pioneering carvers Edwin Kasko, Carl Heinmiller, Jenny Lyn Smith, Warren Price, and Leo Jacobs Sr. And at the Alaska Pavilion for the 1970 World's Fair in Japan, villagers from Kake built Alaska's and maybe the world's tallest properly sanctioned totem pole.

Throughout the 1970s, the Department of the Interior Indian Arts and Crafts Board sponsored workshops for Tlingit and Haida carvers. The apprentice system was revived at the Totem Heritage Center in Ketchikan, culminating in offering the modern Certificate of Merit in Carving, based on the university model of fine art courses. An apprentice system and classes were also instituted at the Southeast Alaska Cultural Center in Sitka. Led by a few gifted artists, a new standard of totem art found its way into Alaska's ferry terminals, government buildings, private collections, and galleries. Carvers such as (non-Native) Greg Horner, (Tlingit) Wayne Price, and (non-Native) John Hagen began their careers during this period. Various artisans who understood the tradition not only began wood carving, but also working with materials such as silver, gold, and glass. Ketchikan's Totem Heritage Center was established in 1976 to house a priceless collection of old totem fragments, and in Sitka, the National Park

Service provided funding for the carving of eight new poles between 1978 and 1986. Carving the first pole cost $4,000, the last $22,000.

Famed Alaska Tlingit carver Nathan Jackson progressed from creating pocketknife carvings with his clan relative Ted Lawrence in the 1950s through an initiation period visiting museum totem collections in New York, attending the Santa Fe School of Indian Art, then dancing and carving with Haines's Carl Heinmiller of Alaska Indian Arts, Inc. Jackson shared in Alaska State Museum kudos with carver Tony Hunt (Kwakwaka'wakw) in 1971, shared expertise with carver Duane Pasco (non-Native master carver), and learned adze skills as well as design fundamentals from art historian Bill Holm. Through these sorts of efforts and more, talented Natives throughout the Pacific Northwest and Alaska were able to relearn traditional forms of Native carving and its attendant ceremonies. Beginning in the 1960s, these enthusiastic and serious young artists and others took advantage of new training opportunities, and the

Tlingit men work on duplicating an old totem at Totem Bight, a project sponsored by the Civilian Conservation Corps in 1939.

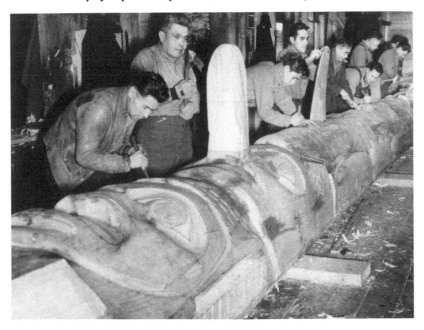

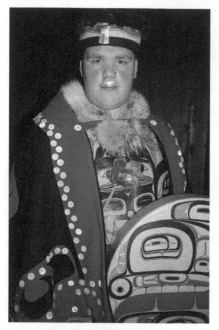

David R. Boxley is among the latest generation of Tsimshian carvers.

general revival of interest in Native American arts and culture of the 1960s reinvigorated traditional arts. These artists were more prolific than the previous generation of carvers and more inclined to push traditional boundaries. With raised interest in Native culture on the part of the public, and more attention from scholars and museum exhibits, the market for contemporary Native art expanded, and it became more possible to earn a living by creating Pacific Northwest Native art.

Throughout the 1980s and 1990s, an increasing number of talented carvers developed both respect and affinity for the traditional art forms. A few old poles were retrieved from museums and carefully restored; new poles were carved for parks and collectors. Alaska steadily produced talented carvers, including Michael and Richard Beasley, David A. Boxley and his son David R. Boxley, Steve Brown, Bruce Cook, Will Burkhart, Darald DeWitt, John Hagen, Jim Heaton, Greg Horner, Joe Jacobs, Nathan Jackson and his son Stephen Jackson, Tommy Joseph, Israel Shotridge and his brother Norman G. Jackson, Ernest Smeltzer, Donny Varnell, and Lee Wallace.

Then in an unusual event in August 2001, under a blazing-hot sun, invited guests gathered at the Pilchuck Glass School in Washington state, famous for its founder-glassmaker Dale Chihuly. There guests bore witness to the raising of the first totem to combine traditional red cedar with cast, etched, and blown glass components, along with the use of neon lighting. Alaska master carvers John Hagen, David Svenson, and others, collaborating with Tlingit glass artist Preston Singletary, raised *The Founders Totem Pole*, to bridge tradition and innovation.

Over the last 50 years, non-Natives also have become increasingly recognized for their contributions, whether it be in analyzing Native art, conducting classes or workshops, giving lectures, or writing articles and books. Academics such as Robin K. Wright, art historian Bill Holm's protégé, and art historian and curator of the Burke Museum in Seattle, represent a long line of caring individuals who have sought to document and preserve totem traditions.

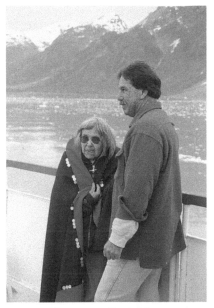

Tlingit carver Frank Fulmer accompanies his mother to Glacier Bay, her family's ancient hunting area.

And so totem lore grows to the present day. In the Native village of Saxman near Ketchikan, a daily parade of tourists files by a stand of totem poles, some 30 and 40 feet tall. In a shed nearby, Tlingit master carver Nathan Jackson, who has been designated a National Living Treasure, wields an adze of Swedish steel. With each swing of his arm, a cedar shaving the size of a fingernail flies off. Jackson works on the totem, detailing exquisite features into a figure that will sit 30 feet above the ground. Despite the modern country music pulsating from the radio in his workshop, the technique of carving totems remains unchanged. He sometimes answers questions.

As a person who has guided emerging carvers for over 30 years, Jackson wants his apprentices to develop an appreciation for their cultural traditions and pass them on to their children and grandchildren. Jackson has studied older poles and learned much from early carvers. "It's too bad we didn't get to see or talk to any of these guys," he says, "because they were pretty good themselves. It'd be dandy to get a critique here or there." Yes, it would be good to hear from them. While their exact words may be lost in time, their wisdom lives on in Alaska's persistent totem tradition. ■

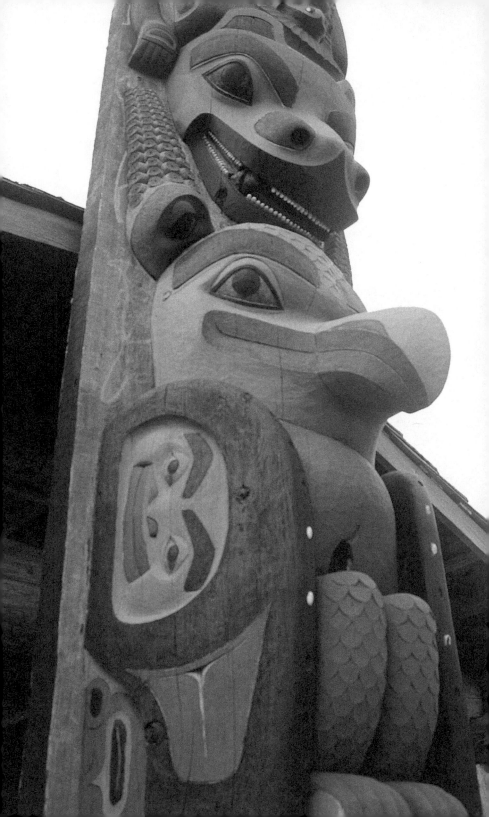

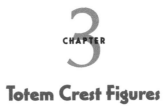

3

Totem Crest Figures

Tribal Carving Styles

In earlier times, there were discernible differences among the totem art styles of the Southeast Alaska tribes. Today, the tradition tends toward ever higher standards of artistry. Traditionally, Haida crest forms, for example, were tightly interlocked in a cylindrical fashion around a pole, with creatures biting one another, grasping a fin, thrusting a tongue, or squatting between the legs or ears of another creature. Beaks or snouts were flattened into a pole's surface. The Haida were noted for their naturalistic representation of human faces, with generously sized eyes formed with two pointed sides. Pole-top eyes focused downward, while lower figures gazed in the general direction of the viewer.

By contrast, traditional Tlingit totem makers carved figures that stood more or less separately from one another, with wings, fins, beaks, and snouts outlined in paint or carved as wood additions. Circular eye pupils with round or pinched edges peered out. In the late 1600s, Tlingit totem carvers no doubt came into contact with the Kaigani Haida, who had arrived from Haida Gwaii

On this Tlingit totem in Hoonah, a smug Raven stands beneath one eye of an Octopus and below Wolf baring its shell teeth.

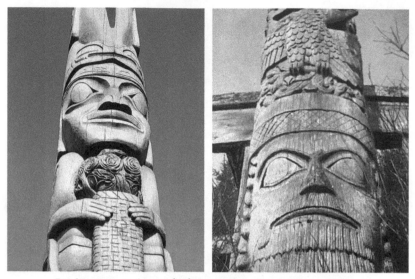

Tsimshian "uninvited guest" (left), in a Metlakatla pole by Stan Marsden,
(Tsimshian) holds a funeral basket of roses. An ancient Haida pole, carved
circa 1880 by Dwight Wallace (Haida) and erected in Howkan, depicts
a bearded Russian trader who was married to a chief's daughter.

(the Queen Charlotte Islands on the British Columbia coast) in a large
migration just before the first encounters with European explorers. As the
two cultures occasionally intermingled and observed each other's styles,
influences flowed in both directions.

The Tsimshian people also arrived from British Columbia to settle
Alaska's Annette Island in the 1880s. They brought their own distinctive
artistic features to pole making, including "portholes" used as house entrances
or used in free-standing totems as story-telling mechanisms, and a band of
tiny clustered figures as a feature representing humanity. Early Tsimshian
carvers living in coastal British Columbia had also come into contact with the
island-dwelling Haida people. Tsimshian traditions were revived in Alaska in
the 1970s, under the notable influence of David A. Boxley, and later his son
David R. Boxley. His diligent research, and the visits of culture bearers who
did exchanges between Alaska and Canada, reenergized the Alaska groups'
songs, dancing, and carving.

Today Alaska's three tribal groups retain many distinct traditional style differences in their totem carving, and with study, the viewer can come to understand the different styles. In the last half century, though, up and down the Pacific Northwest Coast, there also has been a crossover of styles, a burgeoning of personalized styles, and a new emphasis on pleasing artistic form as individual Native carvers find their own aesthetic directions.

Color on Totems

Since the earliest explorers arrived, it was noted that some totem poles had applied colors while others did not. Presumably a man with an eye for color, French explorer Capt. Etienne Marchand's writer C.P. Fleurieu, reported that the totems he saw in 1791 were of a "vibrant red, black, and apple green"—a remarkably precise description for that era. Today, whether a totem has color or not is a decision made by the carver and the tradition he is following. Certain carvers leave the carved cedar trunk unpainted, allowing it to transform to

Rare old Tlingit totem (left) in Wrangell was colored with natural paints, muted by age and wear. Modern Tlingit totem at Totem Bight (right) was painted with house paint.

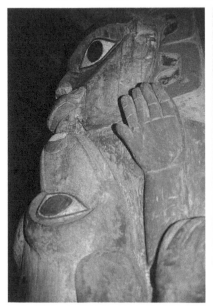
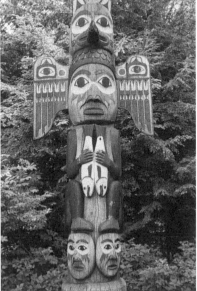

a natural silver gray color, just as human hair does. Others paint on a few highlights, while still others paint every available surface.

Traditionally, the pigments used for totem poles were limited to hues of red, black, or blue green. Traditional colors originally appeared as opaque paints when new, and eventually faded to semitransparent stains. Red ochre, a naturally occurring iron oxide mineral rock, was crushed to form red powder; crushed celanonite nodules made green; yellow ochre was useful; and either charcoal or graphite, an earth pigment, made black. A form of white clay came from Prince of Wales Island. To create bonding agents for these colors, the ground powders were blended with the oils from chewed salmon or trout eggs. Two rare examples of early painted totems are on display inside Chief Shakes's house in Wrangell. These posts were once painted fully, and even with weathering, staining on the wood remains. Ever since carvers could barter with a ship's carpenter, colors have been applied using paints formulated or manufactured by non-Natives.

Among today's Haida, Tlingit, and Tsimshian carvers, almost all of them paint at least the basic highlights of faces—eyes, eyebrows, mouths, and noses. They may leave the background unpainted or paint the entire pole. It's according to personal preference, says Tsimshian carver and culture bearer David A. Boxley. Painted totem poles need regular maintenance to keep colored surfaces bright, though old totems with fading colors have a certain charm. On totems that are painted, black is applied to the primary outlines, red is for secondary elements, and blue or blue green for tertiary areas. Individual Alaska carvers may add sienna, yellow, white, brown, green, or light blue. Totems are painted naturalistically—teeth white, animal furs brown or black, claws black, tongues red, and eyes white with black centers. Creatures such as Thunderbird and Sea Wolf may display a wide range of colors, for who is to say what their true colors really are.

Totem Crests

For the Pacific Northwest Coast Indians, in a time not long ago there was a parallel reality superimposed upon the world in which ordinary humans dwell. Without realizing it, a human might step into or out of this world. Or during a hunt, a human might slay an animal from this alternate existence, put on its skin, and gain supernatural powers. The alternate reality, existing within

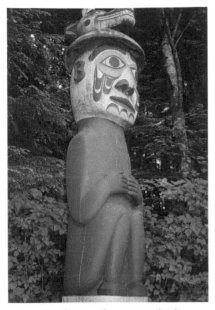

In this Tlingit replica memorial pole, the crouching man wears a Bear hat with Whales painted on the brim.

three realms—the sky world, underwater world, and land world—seemed strangely like home. But the creatures were old-fashioned, living life as humans did before contact. In this place, transformation is a key power. Spirit-creatures had the ability to turn into humans, into other animals, or even into objects such as pine needles or rocks. Time was distorted and the dead didn't always remain dead. Ordinary people lost their fears, had the ability to cure other's wounds and illnesses, could be instantly transported to different areas, and became quite attached to the supernatural residents who lived there. Once trapped there, a human began to forget his or her ordinary life. If the human did manage to return home, he or she became a hero with authorized emblems (or "crests") that were then passed on to descendants and displayed on their totem poles.

Family groups, or clans, officially acquired new crests when certain conditions were met. Crests were owned by lineages or clans by virtue of a special historical or spiritual event or encounter. When that event was memorialized, it was then represented by a symbol, publicly unveiled, and installed at a public ceremony. Some of Alaska's sanctioned crests listed below are widely used among today's Tlingit, Haida, and Tsimshian peoples; others appear less frequently.

Totem Stories

Stories associated with totem crests, passed along within the oral tradition, are subject to variances as they are repeated over and over again. Each time they are retold, the current social conditions, beliefs, and linguistic relationship

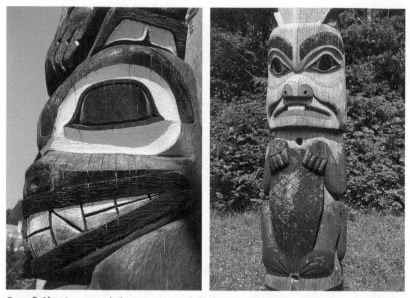

Bear (left) in Juneau with sharp incisor teeth displays distinctive Tlingit blue-green color. Tlingit Beaver at Saxman Totem Park (right) holds its crosshatched tail.

of the tellers and the listeners are likely to cause variations ranging from slightly different nuances to deviations in plot and content. Sometimes characters from one clan's stories are renamed and perhaps even subttly integrated into another clan's story. In the past, specific stories associated with a clan's totem were considered to be owned by that clan.

Early ethnographers collected various totem lore. John Reed Swanton (1873–1958), American anthropologist, collected stories at Sitka and Wrangell in 1904. Ethnographer, photographer, and collector George T. Emmons's (1852–1945) collection of papers on the Tlingit people compiled from 1903 to about 1930 was put into final form for publishing after his death. Several later ethnographers and scholars listed in this book's Further Reading wrote down versions of the stories they heard from the 1940s to the 1970s and up to the present.

BEAR AND BEAR MOTHER. Bear, presumably the brown bear or grizzly, not the black bear, is a figure usually recognized by its sharp canine teeth, somewhat pointed snout, large round nostrils, long curved claws, and flat-topped ears. Bear sometimes exhibits a protruding tongue. Bear Mother may hold one or both of her twin cubs in her paws or perhaps within her eyes or ears. She or her cubs can confusingly appear as humans. Bear may be depicted squatting on its haunches, or in full animal profile sitting horizontally on top of a shaft sometimes incised with bear claw marks. Also known as Xóots, Kaiti, or Grizzly among the Haida, and the subject of several stories, Bear interacts enthusiastically with humans and has a special affinity for marrying human chief's pretty daughters, often becoming the ancestor of a human Bear family.

THE ORIGIN OF KILLER WHALE

The skilled hunter Naatsilanéi once went spear fishing with his ever-jealous brothers-in-law. In spite of the protestations of the youngest, his resentful in-laws purposely abandoned him, silently gliding off in their dugout canoe. Finding himself alone, Naatsilanéi administered first aid to an ailing seagull, who gratefully introduced him to the Sea Lions. In their underwater village, he spotted the chief's son, ailing from the very wound that Naatsilanéi had inflicted on him earlier that day. In return for healing his son, the Sea Lion Chief presented Naatsilanéi with the gift of an inflatable sea lion skin. Crawling inside, our hero floated back to his village and cunningly crept home for his tools. Back on the beach, he carved eight Killer Whale figures, first from alder, then spruce, then hemlock. But when he carved them from yellow cedar, they drifted out to sea, animated into living Whales, and returned with fish for him. Thus fortified, he instructed the Whales to kill his brothers-in-law, save for the youngest, which they did. After this nasty deed, Naatsilanéi instructed them to never again harm humans. This they mostly obeyed, although because of their yellow cedar origins, whale fat crackles in a fire just like wood.

(Ethnographer Marius Barbeau (1883–1969) attributes one version of this story to documentation by American anthropologist Viola E. Garfield (1899–1983), best known for her work on the social organization the Tsimshian nation in British Columbia and Alaska. She collected it in the 1930s regarding a totem at the village of Tuxekan, Alaska. Throughout the 1920s and 1930s, H. P. Corser, a member of the American School of Archeology, collected totem stories throughout Alaska. Walter C. Waters, the owner of a pharmacy store in Wrangell, published several of Corser's stories, including this one, in 1940.) ●

In Tlingit lore, Kâts is a human hunter who succumbs to the seductive allure of a she-Bear and leaves behind a grieving human wife. In both the Haida and the Tlingit version of this story, the transformation of Bear from animal to human is assumed in order to understand the story. Indoors, Bear takes off his/her bearskin coat and acts like a human being—living as a member of an extended family in a community clan house. In human form Bear can marry a real human and have offspring. These human-animal unions produce children who sometimes appear as humans and sometimes as bear cubs.

BEAVER. According to ethnographer and folklorist Marius Barbeau (1883–1969), Tsimshian and Haida groups used the Beaver figure to display their rights to engage in the lucrative fur trade. With two bucked incisor teeth in front, its tail crosshatched and displayed in the front of the animal, some Haida Beavers hold a stick or an arrow in their teeth or between their two front paws. If the arrow is broken, it is said to symbolize peace after a war—usually a pelt trade war between clans. Considered malicious creatures that could chisel murderous arrows, some Beavers were said to tunnel under villages or slap their huge tails causing earthquakes or landslides. Called Tsing by one Haida clan, by chanting a song one Beaver could change snowy weather into warm misty rain. Also in certain Haida stories, Beaver was once one of Raven's uncles, who long ago lived on the floor of the sea where he hoarded all the fresh water and fish of the world.

The Killisnoo Beaver of the Angoon Tlingit had a magical tail with a face. If a person wanted this Beaver to die, the face had to be killed separately. In another Tlingit story from the Sitka and Wrangell area, documented by Swanton, Beaver was a friend of Porcupine. Since Bear could break his dam and eat Beaver but was afraid of Porcupine's quills, as a protective measure Beaver invited Porcupine to stay in his lodge. One day hungry Porcupine left to climb trees to find tender twigs, sap, bark, and needles. But when Beaver, following his friend, managed to climb a nearby tree to escape Bear, he became trapped. As Porcupine lumbered away to continue eating, it was Squirrel who eventually coaxed Beaver down. Next Porcupine unwisely swam after Beaver into the middle of a lake. There he became stranded on an island. Now it was Beaver's turn to ignore his friend. In despair, Porcupine sang for the Wolverine, who had influence with the North Wind. The wind froze the lake so the prickly one

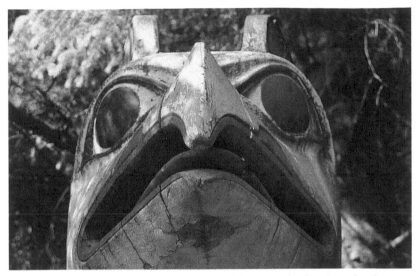

An Eagle at Totem Bight Historical State Park has its eyes fixed on the realm of the sky world, which, according to Tlingit stories, preoccupies the bird.

could walk home. In this way, because of their different lifestyles, Beaver and Porcupine's friendship also cooled.

BLACKFISH. Today known as Killer Whale or Orca, this figure is recognized on totems by its dark fish-shaped body, dorsal fin, and blowhole. Interestingly, the blowhole can be found almost anywhere on the body from the forehead area to inside the dorsal fin. Various Killer Whale representations are found among all Southeast Alaska's totem tribes.

An illustrative historical incident involving a Whale crest took place in the late 1700s along the Stikine (sti-KEEN) River, located in northwestern British Columbia and flowing into southeastern Alaska where it drains into the Alexander Archipelago. The Nishga people of the Tsimshian Nation, a clan group called Wiisheyksh (referring to the sound of a surfacing killer whale), which used Whale as their crest, demanded access to the Stikine and the food supplies associated with it. The Tlingit, called the Naanya.aayi, who controlled the river, refused, and prepared for war. More than 100 canoes of Nishga warriors are said to have approached the mouth of the river. A battle ensued. After hard-fought combat, the Naanya.aayi were victorious and the Wiisheyksh were forced to capitulate. Not wishing to become slaves of the victors, the leader of the Wiisheyksh, who was wearing a headdress with the Killer Whale emblem, removed his headdress and offered it to Gush X'een, the Tlingit clan's representative. Placing it on his head, Gush X'een said, "Not only do I take your hat, I take your name as well." So it was that the name of Wiisheyksh became a Tlingit name and was shortened to Sheiyksh, now called Shakes (or Sheiks, pronounced as one "shakes" his head). The storied descendants of that victorious representative, the Shaikes (or Shakes) chiefs, went on to become a significant family with ties to present-day Wrangell. Since that time, Killer Whale has appeared head-down on British Columbia totem poles, signaling defeat among those Nishga people who lost the battle, while a horizontal or heads-up posture, sometimes exhibited in Alaska, is said to indicate this long-ago victory.

SOOTY SKIN, OR DUK-TOOTHL

A huge Sea Lion had killed the best hunter in the village. Seeking revenge, the deceased hunter's uncles organized a plan. All their nephews were to go into training. The young men were required to bathe in cold saltwater and beat themselves with branches to build up their endurance. But one nephew refused to train. Thought to be lazy, he was normally curled up asleep in the ashes beside the fire. Soon he was scorned for his sooty skin and mockingly called Duk-toothl. At night, however, this young man secretly built up his strength and learned to hold his breath underwater. The day of the contest, the nephews prepared for battle. Because everyone belittled him, Duk-toothl had to beg to attend. After all the young men have failed, our hero dove underwater, chased a sea lion, captured it, then ripped it in half. Those who were cruel to him were now fearful of the boy's strength. Duk-toothl did not take revenge on his tormentors, but instead forgave them, thus showing his strength of character, as well as of body.

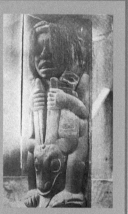

Historic totem with human hair shows Duk-toothl tearing a sea lion in half.

(First collected by anthropologist John R. Swanton about 1909 and published in *Tlingit Myths and Texts*, author Edward L. Keithahn again collected this Tlingit story in Wrangell and published it in 1946. Marius Barbeau repeated it in his book, *Totem Poles*, 1950.) ●

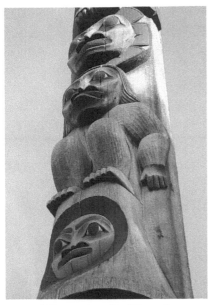

A Tlingit girl in a Ketchikan pole appears under Sun and above a figure (probably Moon) on Raven's hat.

In the spirit world, Blackfish live in underwater villages, where (depending on the clan stories, especially among the Haida people) they fraternize with a number of powerful underwater supernatural spirit humans such as Copper Woman. Killer Whale can capture a canoe, drag it under water, and transform its occupants into Killer Whales. Sometimes, a Killer Whale near the shore is a transformed human, trying to communicate with his family. Rare totems display the crests of the mythic Double- or Triple-finned Killer Whale. Also in an oft-told Haida story and popular subject for plays, also adopted by the Tlingit people, Nanasimget, a mere human, tells the entangled adventures of a man who once rode a Killer Whale down to its underwater domain desperately seeking his kidnapped wife.

EAGLE, THUNDERBIRD, AND KADJUK. On totems, Eagle is recognizable as a bird with a prominent curved, hooked beak. Notable as a totem-topper, sometimes with outstretched wings and sometimes not, Eagle can in fact appear anywhere on a totem. Thunderbird, a mighty supernatural eagle-like creature common to several indigenous cultures of North America, is rarely used by the Tlingit and Haida, though it does appear on a Haida totem in Totem Bight State Historical Park. It is reputed to protect humans or restore justice by fighting evil. Thunderbird is similar in appearance to Eagle, although it is often shown with curled appendages on top of the head and with a recurved upper beak like a hawk. The legendary and powerful Kadjuk, a Teikweidi Tlingit crest perched atop a tall pole, is the representation of a huge eagle-like spirit-raptor from lofty domains. Kadjuk hunts by dropping stones on unsuspecting marmots.

Eagle houses as part of the phratry system and as clan crests are found among the Haida, Tsimshian, and Tlingit peoples. Eagles are liberally depicted in the official coats of arms of Imperial Russia, Great Britain, Germany, and the United States.

In its totem stories, Eagle is generally preoccupied with its own sky kingdom, though occasionally during highly charged moments will take notice of the human realm. Once during a terrible plague, a certain Mother Eagle brought fish to a starving girl and her grandmother. When it feels hungry, some Eagles are said to pull on a cloak of feathers and search for Whales or Giant Woodworms, its favorite foods. It is also rumored that these raptors will lift roof beams into place during house construction for their favorite clansmen.

According to some Tsimshian stories, only a few humans have ever made it to the spirit sky realm where Eagle lives. A flock of geese, acting like helium balloons, have flown a few lucky humans up to where Eagle and Thunderbird rule. But others who wished to commune with these gigantic raptors have had to climb high into the mountains to wait for a thunderstorm to sweep them up into the sky kingdom. Some Haida clans say that lightning is produced as Thunderbird blinks its angry golden eyes; others say it's a dart from Thunderbird's serpent-like tongue. In other stories, thunder is said to originate from the beating of the Thunderbird's enormous wings.

According to Swanton, the Tlingit from Wrangell tell one story about a man who married an Eagle, though qualifying it as something that happened among the Haida. A fugitive on the run fixed upon a plan to take a large seal, skin it, hide himself inside the skin, and set himself adrift. Next morning, an Eagle landed on top of the butchered seal. The man took out his knife, cut through the skin, and seized its legs. Lo, instead of an eagle, there was a girl, who invited him to her father's house, where she became his wife. As a wedding present each of his Eagle in-laws presented him with different coats. Informing him that upon wearing their gifts, he would be able to catch various fish and seals, he did so. During his forays aloft, he spied a lonely old woman who had been sent away to die on a faraway beach. He shared some of his catch with her. Ultimately, becoming protective of the elder, he saved her, and in the form of a great Eagle himself, destroyed the men in the village.

FROG. Frog may appear alone on a totem, emerging from the mouth or ears of another creature or wedged between other forms. Looking like its animal counterpart, with its broad toothless mouth, big eyes, and in a crouched position, Frog is easy to identify. In some Tlingit stories, the Frog People have encounters with people whose descendants are then variously gifted to understand Frogs more fully. On one Saxman Park totem, frog heads peek up from receding lake waters. And on a famous ridicule totem pole in Wrangell, three Frogs represent the clan designations of the three people being singled out for humiliation over a debt.

In one Kiksa'di Tlingit story from Wrangell, documented by Swanton, the town-chief's daughter made fun of the many Frogs that sat in the lake: "There are so many of these creatures, I wonder if they do things like human beings. I wonder if men and women cohabit among them." That night, a

RAVEN LIBERATES THE SUN, MOON, AND STARS

Raven was going along one day when he spied a great clan house and a beautiful girl beside it. She was drawing water. This was in the time-before-now when there were no stars or planets, no tides or animals as we know them, and it was twilight all the time. Wandering around after having recently burned himself black in a fire and hungry as usual, he was restless. But the girl's father knew of clever Raven, so his house was closely guarded. Crafty Raven therefore transformed himself into a pine needle ready to float down the stream. When the girl

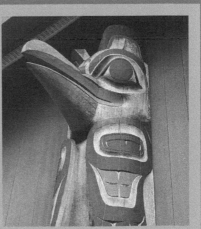

Mischievous Raven tops
this Tlingit pole.

next came to fetch water, she took a drink and swallowed the pine needle. She soon gave birth to a precocious son who ate constantly and shrieked mercilessly. He begged for the bentwood box full of twinkling stars hidden in the corner. When the stars flew up the smoke hole, he pretended to be sorry. Next he demanded the silvery Moon ➤

strange young man proposed marriage to her. She agreed to go to his home under the lake, where she soon lost the memory of her former life. In vain, her father and friends searched for her and finally gave up. The following spring, a young man spotted her sitting among the Frogs. In spite of her father's negotiations, the Frogs would not release her. Eventually, the villagers dug a trench to drain the lake, scattering Frogs everywhere. Home at last, the chief's daughter made the popping noise *Hu*, like a frog makes. She could not eat properly, so her family hung her over a pole to drain the black mud out of her. Alas, she died. The Frogs in that place now understand human beings very well. And some of the people almost understand Frog too. They also possess Frog songs, Frog personal names, and a Frog crest.

LAND MONSTERS. Left over from a time long ago when cannibals ruled the world, there are hushed stories of fearsome Giants and various Land

RAVEN LIBERATES THE SUN, MOON, AND STARS continued

that hung on the wall, and though his grandfather objected, his mother gave in. Flicking the Moon up through the smoke hole, it flew into the sky while Raven screeched in delight. Next he whined for the box his grandfather kept hidden under his bed. Day after day, he would not stop complaining until his mother relented, planning to guard it closely. Quickly Raven threw himself and the box into the fire, escaped on the updraft, and resumed his bird form.

"Fetch me some food and drink," he demanded of everyone he met, "for I own something wonderful." But they mocked him. With a thundering flash he threw open the box, and the Sun flew into the heavens. Those who were wearing animal skins became animals forevermore, and those who were naked became humans. And that is how sun, moon, and stars came to be in the heavens.

(In the 1870s, Haida carver Albert Edward Edenshaw related this Raven story to accompany a totem he made for the Haida, though both the Tlingit and Tsimshian traditions claim many early Raven stories. Early ethnographers and anthropologists collected this rendition several more times: Franz Boas in 1902, John R. Swanton about 1910, William Benyon in 1922, and Edward L. Keithahn circa 1930. Marius Barbeau included it in his 1950 book, *Totem Poles*, attributing one version to an old Haida sea captain, Andrew Brown, who told this now-familiar version to him in 1939.) ●

Monsters. Of the so-called Wild Men—the thick-skinned Goo-teekhl and Gootz-hun, ferocious human figures—these ancient Tlingit emblems are the focus of stories rarely published. In the forest north of Klukwan in Tlingit territory, there once lived a cannibal so huge he was the terror of all the Chilkat country. When this creature was finally captured and burned, his ashes flew up into the air to be transformed into little gray insects with a taste for blood. With its pointy proboscis, Mosquito, a monster-sized likeness on some totems, is the result. There is one totem pole on the side of the Governor's Mansion in Juneau portraying Mosquito.

The Kooshdaakáa or Land Otter Man is also a Tlingit creature, while the Gagixit is a Haida Wild Man. Land Otter People, usually Tlingit in origin, are creatures described as giant humans covered in fur but on totems appear like their namesake, otters. They have the ability to make themselves invisible, and in many stories, especially from Yukatut and Sitka, they have a yen for kidnapping humans. Given the absence of a drowned body, the soul of a dead person might be consigned to the form of a Land Otter Man who wandered in an eternal abyss. Years later their pathetic victims, if found, could only grovel about on hands and knees.

Woodworm, an out-of-control pet, in Tlingit stories is depicted as a giant segmented worm person. In the stories of the Gaanaxteidi Tlingit of Klukwan, after an innocent girl befriends one and secretly feeds it cooking oil, it becomes large enough that it threatens the village and the men have to kill it with wooden spears.

LOON. Sometimes depicted as a man or a woman with bird features, Loon can also be shown more realistically as a bird, especially among the Haida where in some stories it features as an important agent in the creation of humans. According to other tales, as the fog rolls in, this melancholy sounding bird delights in frightening humans on the shore or in their canoes, and its repetitive call often succeeds in annoying folks. In Tlingit lore, as recorded by George T. Emmons, a woman mimics a loon.

OTTER. Not to be confused with the fearsome Land Otter Man, which is usually associated with shamans in Tlingit lore, Otter is a Haida figure. In a story reported by Marius Barbeau, once when Raven was traveling the

Haida world, he came across a man sharpening a spear with which to kill him. He turned the man into Otter (like the river otter) and the spear became its tail.

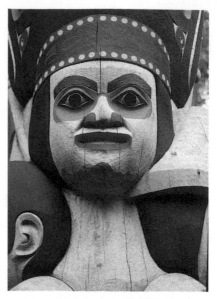

OWL. Resembling a barn owl with its tightly curled beak and large round eyes, Owl is a figure that once lived on the earth either as a man or a wife with in-law. One Kiksadi Tlingit story from Sitka tells of a married couple. It should be understood that in extended families, mothers-in-law often came to live with the couple as part of the marriage arrangement. In this instance, the man's wife refused to give her mother-in-law any herring to eat. After she had refused her

A contemporary Tlingit pole by Nathan Jackson (Tlingit) stands at Ketchikan's Totem Heritage Center.

twice, she spitefully placed hot milt (fish spawn) into her mother-in-law's hand and burned it. For this reason, her son took out the canoe, filled it with herring by means of a herring rake, and upon his return bade his wife to bring the herring up to the house. "Bring down the basket," his wife cried. "Don't listen to her," her husband instructed the household. Night came on and still she begged. Toward morning the sound of the woman's cries began to change, *Hû, hû, hû, û.* Her husband then said to her, "You can become an Owl from this time on." As she transformed and flew off, he informed her, "You put milt into my mother's hand. For that you can become a screech Owl." The story goes on to say, this is why we can understand the owl: it always predicts bad weather, and it tells what is going to happen in other towns.

RAVEN. A pivotal crest figure for all three tribes, for the Tsimshian the Ganhada (variously spelled) is the name for the Raven "clan" (phratry), while among Tlingit people, the two great moieties are Raven (Yéil) and Eagle/Wolf

(Ch'aak'/Gooch.) Raven, with assorted descriptive names, is also one of the two great phratries or clans into which the Haida are divided. This legendary creature is a powerful trickster who appears in countless traditional stories. Raven is a mischievous bird spirit capable of transformation into all manner of forms, such as animals, humans, or even objects as simple as a pine needle. He has a prominent long, blunt beak, and through his stories is credited with causing most of the well-known phenomena in nature. Raven is so powerful he occasionally appears on totems with symbols of high rank such as a Chilkat blanket or a basketry hat topped with rings. Though in stories he maliciously breaks the rules of nature, Raven's impish antics usually prove to have beneficial effects for ordinary humans. On at least a dozen Tlingit totems in Alaska, Raven appears with Sun or stands on the bentwood box from which he is said to have liberated the Sun, the light of the world.

Raven lives in the sky realm, in some traditions along with his slaves Gitsanuk and Gitsaqeq, though he is often found somewhere on earth greedily searching for food or discovering shiny objects. Ever curious and naughty, it is said in some stories that it was Raven who led his Tlingit people to their new homeland when they first arrived in Alaska.

SEA MONSTERS. Ocean-living monsters with war-like qualities seem to be designed from two creatures morphed into one. The Sea Bear, with its alternating whale features and bear parts, occupies the underwater realm with Sea Wolf, also known as Wasgo. Both Sea Bear and Sea Wolf are wealth-bringing creatures. Though Sea Wolf may appear with a combination of wolf paws and whale fins, it does not have a Killer Whale fin, just a tall dorsal fin. Stories claim it has several more unusual transformations. Furiously shedding water droplets, Sea Wolf can also sport coppery wing-like appendages, or suddenly rise from the sea. It can mysteriously appear as an elaborately painted war canoe, or even as a beautifully painted house, inlaid with blue and green shells and topped with the head of an immense fish. Both American and German submarine corps have apparently been inspired by this stealthy totem creature—the powerful Sea Wolf.

SPIRIT WOMEN. To the Ketchikan-area Tlingit, Fog Woman, also known to the Haida as Bright-Cloud Woman, is a totem story figure depicted with a saucer-shaped hat and recognized as a human woman of high rank with a labret or lip plug—a symbol of aristocracy. According to one Tlingit story she was briefly married to the great and powerful Raven, though she left him because he was such a poor provider. But before she departed, she first learned a powerful skill. Forced to beg for herself and her daughters, she discovered that upon turning her magical spruce-root hat upside down, all the fogs and mists would enter it, leaving the sky clear and bright. Fog Woman's daughters, the Creek Women, are beauties, depicted as human girls, who live at the head of every stream and protect the salmon. It is the ultimate joy of a salmon's life to fight its way upstream for one look at these lovely young women. In Haida stories, Fog Woman is an ambitious socialite, friend of Frog, and in other stories is married to the noble Prince of Bears.

She's far different from the vengeful Tsimshian Foam Woman, a whirlpool monster depicted as a devouring woman with a big mouth, feared by warriors even when they are paddling in their sturdiest war canoes.

At Saxman near Ketchikan, Giant Rock Oyster holds the unfortunate Tlingit person who dared taunt him.

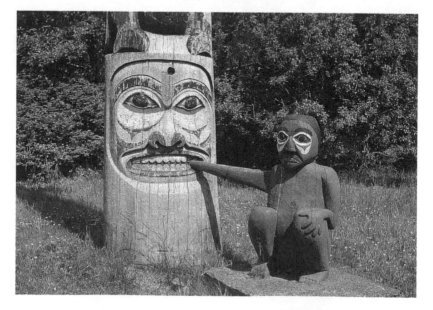

UNDERWATER ANIMALS AND MARINE LIFE. On Tlingit totems, the local octopus, traditionally called Devilfish, is sometimes depicted tentacles and all. Clam is also a totem figure, and appears in a few stories. For both Devilfish and Clam, the stories portray the destructive tendencies of these creatures. In one case, a Devilfish destroys a number of canoes and an entire town, and in another, Clam holds a person's hand fast in its grip until the tide drowns him.

Bullhead, a fish-like figure with whiskers, appears in Raven stories and on a few totem poles. Beginning as a beautiful white fish and outwitted by Raven, it ends up as a skinny, bony creature. Sculpin, an ancient Haida totem crest, takes its name from a tiny fish found in Alaskan waters. Recognizable for its flat spikes, the sculpin fish's pointy bones were traditionally made into armor plate. In stories, any human who pressed into these spines suffered horribly. At Sitka, one Haida pole, believed to be a crest pole portraying the emblems of the Yaadaas clan, depicts a flawed human, Lakich'inei, with one of his children, who is half human and half dog. Sea Lion has a broad head, with or without teeth or ears, with fore and hind flippers and a triangular shaped tail, and features in some stories about a strong man.

Dogfish, also known as Shark or Mud Shark, with a crescent-shaped mouth, is a particularly striking crest that was once depicted on utilitarian household objects and on a few totem poles. It has a flat look and crescent-shaped gill slits. Dogfish may be portrayed with a labret inserted in its lip, the reminder of a noblewoman who Dogfish carried off long ago. On Haida totems, particularly those depicted by culture bearer and Haida carver Bill Reid, she is also Dogfish Woman, an upper-class woman with a labret, gill slits on her forehead, and a prim crown, a shape-changing creature who is part human and part shark. A rarely obtained spirit, those who gain this shark's favor can sing chants and become skillful dancers.

Halibut is depicted as a large flatfish and is recognized by both eyes being on the upper side of its body. The Tlingit say some of the outlying islands took their present shape when Halibut grew to an enormous size and broke up into little islands. The crashing of its tail scattered people all around. The powerful Prince of Halibut also makes an appearance in a few stories.

Salmon beings live in underwater villages though they seem to retain their fish-like personalities even when encountering humans. If a human eats a Salmon underwater, its bones immediately reassemble and it swims away. A figure holding a shrimp or a crab in its mouth is significant in Haida culture; both are regarded as symbols of thievery.

Sea Lion People appear seal-like in shape in Tlingit lore. Unreliable as friends, they either assist humans who have stumbled into the underwater world or kill them mercilessly. After one such murder in a Tlingit story, they were required to make their peace with Duk-toothl, a young

GONAKADET, THE SEA WOLF

A Tlingit man once loved his dear wife, but his mother-in-law was constantly berating him for his failures as a hunter. One day, he spotted Gonakadet, a fearsome Sea Wolf known to bring luck. Cunningly trapping and skinning the creature, he donned its skin. Thus garbed, he could not be recognized. Unwilling to tell lest his enemies steal the skin, he wore it fishing. Not only did our hero catch a fish for his wife, he secretly left a huge fish as a gift for his mother-in-law. She was delighted, but not knowing who had given her the gift, continued to criticize him for sleeping all day. The next night he left her two more fish, then three, then four, and so on. Soon the mother-in-law claimed she was divine and could predict how many fish would appear. Morning after morning, the household stood amazed as ever-greater quantities of fish appeared. Everyone in the household was well fed. In time, she bragged that she would be gifted with a whale. By now, our hero was exhausted. He took his wife aside to tell her, "If you find something peculiar, be kind." Next morning, intermingled with the dead whale was a strange monster with copper claws, a big head, two fins, and a curly tail. The wife peeked inside the monster's mouth and spotted her husband. She scooped up his body and the skin, and took them to a secret location. No more fish or whales appeared and the villagers turned on the old woman. "Your bragging killed our savior," they complained, and she was shamed to death. His grieving wife put the dry, cracking skin into the lake, and it reanimated. "Onto my back," her transformed husband cried. And the two of them lived forever in a beautiful house with the Daughters of Creeks.

(Journalist James Deans collected a version of this story published in 1889. Anthropologist J. R. Swanton collected a variation in about 1913, as did Edward L. Keithahn around 1946. H. P. Corser, a member of the American School of Archeology, collected totem stories throughout Alaska. Walter C. Waters, the owner of a pharmacy store in Wrangell, published several of his stories, including this one, in 1940. It continues to be told.) •

man developing his physical strength. To show his prowess he ripped a Sea Lion in half.

WHITE PERSONS. The first and only President Lincoln figure carved on top of a totem pole came from Tongass Island near Alaska's southern border shortly after the Alaska purchase in 1867. The original figure resembles the famous president with his stovepipe hat. A small band of Tlingit, seeking sanctuary with a garrison of American soldiers, learned about Lincoln and his efforts to end slavery. In response, a carver named Thele-da reputedly produced a President Lincoln figure for the top of a totem. Today, a fragment in the Alaska State Museum is the only known piece of the original pole that appears in historical photos of Tongass village. There is a CCC so-called replica of this pole displayed in the totem park at Saxman. However, the stovepipe-hatted man is generic in nature. The clan puts forth a different interpretation for the figure on this pole: They claim the white man as a crest, probably because they saw the first European explorers in their area and claimed them as a crest as they would any other noticeable creature.

Bearded human figures considered to be white persons appear on a few totems. One Tlingit totem has epaulets, buttons, and pockets, suggesting a military person who could be an American or Russian officer. Some say the Eagle crest near this figure is copied from old American coins, while others say it is an Imperial Russian Eagle landing on his head to humiliate him. The Imperial Russian eagle has two heads. In another case, the bearded person is a trader the carver decided to ridicule for not paying his debts.

.

WOLF. With a head longer and narrower than that of Bear, it has a long nose, canine teeth, long ears, and in some cases a long tail. In spite of the few recorded Wolf stories among Alaska tribes, many are remembered and passed on within Wolf lineages. Wolf has a longer snout than Bear but the same canine teeth, and often sits crouched on its haunches. Generally, Wolf is depicted with ears that are taller, more pointed than those of Bear. According to a Yukatat native and recorded by George T. Emmons, Raven, having made women for men to marry, then tried to create a "brotherhood" of all the creatures of the world. But Wolf was against him and destroyed the harmonious scheme. So Raven doomed him to wander forever, howling for help. ∎

Frequently Asked Questions about Totem Poles

What do totems mean? Traditionally, a totem pole portrayed inherited crests signifying the entitlements and rank of a related group of people. Because totems are now also carved for outsiders, totem poles have evolved to represent a combination of traditional elements, Native pride, and whatever the master carver and the owners agree that they represent.

Is it possible to "read" a totem pole? Anyone with an understanding of crests can recognize many totem figures. But it is impossible to fully interpret a totem pole's meaning without knowing the history of the family that owns it.

Were old totems constructed to honor tribal ancestors? No. Old totem poles were primarily a record of an entire clan's kinship status, rights, achievements, and deeds with an occasional heroic migration story indicating how their village came to be in its present location. There were, however, memorial totems for specific individuals that portrayed all his crests.

Were totems worshipped? No. Like a country's flag, they were treated with respect.

This clan house entryway in Wrangell displays a painted Bear that
was Tlingit Chief Charles Jones Shakes's clan crest about 1940.

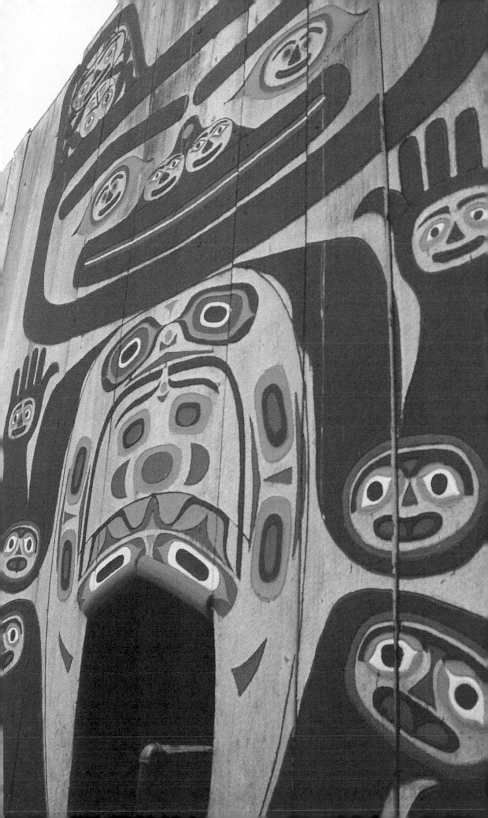

Do totems bring good luck? No, totems are neither talismans nor charms.

What's the difference between totemism and totem poles? Totemism is a belief that certain qualities imparted to an object, such as a stone in the shape of an animal, can be shared with the human who owns the object. Southwest desert-dwelling Zuni people reflect this tradition in fetishes called "animal totems." Though an Alaska totem can convey goodwill, it does not protect anyone.

Do totem poles have anything to do with Freud's "totem"? Sigmund Freud, father of psychoanalysis, discussed a symbolic object of worship protected by taboos, the "totem," as the representation of hidden guilt within the human psyche. Freud's interpretation has nothing to do with the Alaska totem tradition.

Are totem poles like coats of arms? The coat of arms of the United States, an eagle holding a shield, branch, and arrows, represents America's marks of distinction. Many European families research their surname to discover their ancestors' coat of arms. In the same way, it can be argued that a totem pole is a symbolic system for displaying and recording its owners' distinctions or stories.

Where did the word "totem" originate? Explorers to Alaska in the late 1700s labeled the monument-like wooden poles they saw as "great wooden images," "large tree entrances," "monumental figures," "carved trees," "house posts," and "pillars." For use in the English language, the largest number of Native words derived from the Native people who were first encountered by white settlers, the eastern Algonquian tribes. In Ojibwa—an Algonquin language—the expression *ototeman* means roughly "he is a relative of mine." French anthropologist Claude Levi-Strauss (1908–) speculated that this was the origin of the word. The word, twisted into "totem," probably spread through North America with Indian traders during the 1800s.

Are there different types of totem poles? Yes. The huge carved wooden figures that Europeans first observed were called greet or welcome figures. Often marking the outer limits of a tribe's territory, they were huge single figure totems of a human or an animal. Some held boxes of human remains. Soon after, explorers encountered interior house posts, territory marker poles, house frontal entrance poles, and heraldic or free-standing

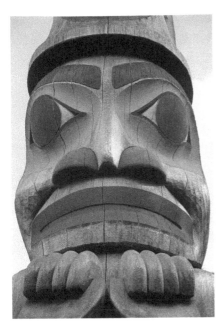

The traditional hat, eyebrows, eyes, nostrils, lips, and fingers indicate this is a human figure.

totems. There were also memorial totem poles and boxes.

Is there such a thing as a "ridicule" pole? Yes, there is a tradition in Alaska of ridiculing others on totems. Sometimes, the crests of apparent thieves or images of bearded white persons were put on display to indicate an unpaid debt.

What are the primary things to look for, in "seeing" a totem pole? To understand what you're looking at on totem poles, it's useful to recognize four characteristic shapes that you will often see in traditional Pacific Northwest Indian totem art: the ovoid, U-shape, split-U, and the elongated S-shape. The ovoid is an oval with flattened corners that can be used alone or as nested ovoids stacked one inside the other. An ovoid often indicates a shoulder, elbow, or knee joint; other times it's a basic space filler. The U-shape is often used for wing feathers and has a rhythmic form often found with the split-U. Rather like a candy kiss, the split-U divides the U-shape in two. The elongated S, used in groups, often depicts an animal's ribs.

Are there extra eyes hidden on totems? Rarely. The ovoid shape used in totem forms is sometimes mistaken for an eye. However, eyes are usually clearly delineated with a pupil and an eyelid that is pinched at both corners.

Are animal body parts sometimes carved out of order? Yes. In certain cases, though more in two-dimensional work than on totem poles, animal or bird figures are split or fragmented, with eyes, joints, legs, fins, wings, or tails appearing out of place. For example, the blowhole for a whale might appear in the center of its dorsal fin.

Are creatures nested inside other creatures on totem poles? Yes. One creature often appears inside another. For example, Bear Mother's cubs can be hidden in her ears, a man can be curled up inside a Whale, or Frog can pop out of a figure's mouth.

Are materials other than wood used in totem poles? Occasionally other materials such as horn, copper, hair, teeth, mirrors, or opercula shells are inlaid for decoration, but these tend to disappear quickly. A recent totem in the state of Washington, carved by sanctioned Alaska carvers, has blown-glass accessories and neon tubing incorporated into it.

Do other aboriginal people make totem poles? Yes. The Ainu people, living on Hokkaido Island in northern Japan, create pole groupings. Some are topped with an animal such as Bear that is sacred to them. And in New Zealand, the Maori people carve house posts said to represent dead ancestors. The first Hawaiians produced totem-like figures called *tikis*. These represented ancestors and were associated with strict taboos. No artistic link has been established among these Pacific Rim peoples, though the possibilities are intriguing.

What are some distinctive features of Alaska totems? Compared with the tribes in British Columbia that practice the totem tradition, Alaska story figures such as Raven Liberating the Sun, Duk-toothl, Gonakadet (Sea Wolf), and Devilfish (Octopus) are portrayed especially expressively. Today, Alaska has several totems that feature vibrant women figures, and Tlingit totems often incorporate a distinctive bright blue-green tertiary color.

Who are some of today's Alaska carvers? Some of Alaska's carvers include David A. Boxley and his son David R. Boxley (Tsimshian), Will Burkhart (Tlingit), Bruce Cook (Haida), Frank L. Fulmer (Tlingit), John Hagen, Wayne Hewson (Tsimshian), Jack Hudson (Tsimshian), Nathan Jackson and his son Stephen Jackson (Tlingit), Norman G. Jackson (Tlingit), Stan Marsden (Tsimshian), Wayne Price (Tlingit), Israel Shotridge (Tlingit), Donny Varnell (Haida), and Lee Wallace (Tlingit).

How old is the totem tradition? It's impossible to know when the Natives of the North Pacific Coast first began to carve and paint crests on their possessions, but the tradition and artistic rendering of clan crests may have evolved over thousands of years. At one dig in British Columbia, archaeologists carbon-dated a 600-year-old bone comb carved with a recognizable

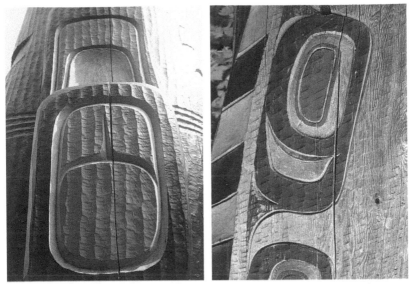

Finishing techniques include feathering (above left) or smoothing with incised
marks (above right), both left by the elbow adze, a primary tool of totem carvers. Below, four
characteristic shapes include the U-shape (left), the elongated-S (right),
the split-U (bottom left), and nested ovoids (bottom right).

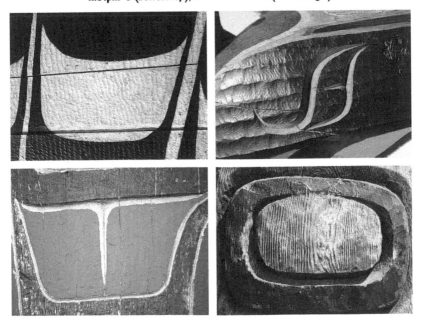

Wolf crest. Alaska's petroglyphs may be older, but stone cannot be carbon-dated.

Do we know the origin of totem poles? No. Before the widespread use of metal tools, Pacific Northwest totem poles were probably fewer and smaller. A traditional item known as a "talking stick" displayed a person's crests. Some speculate that talking sticks evolved into totem poles.

From what type of wood are totems made? The preferred material is Western red cedar, a wood that carves easily yet holds its edge for many years. Some totems are made from Alaska yellow cedar, a similar type of wood. A few are made from Sitka spruce, which is tougher and more difficult to carve.

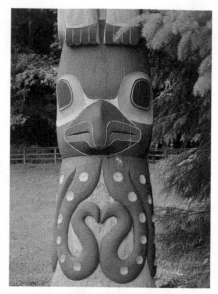

Totem Bight's collection includes this Tlingit Octopus, once known as Devilfish, with tentacles and sucker cups.

How old is an average totem pole? Unless totems have been treated with resistant chemicals or have been sheltered indoors, after 60 to 100 years most totems begin to decompose. They eventually fall over, decay, and return to the earth.

Where are the oldest totem poles located? The oldest and largest collection of totem fragments in Alaska is housed in the Totem Heritage Center in Ketchikan, Alaska. The 33 fragments in this collection, considered invaluable for research purposes, are about 100 years old. The collections of the University of British Columbia Museum of Anthropology in Vancouver, British Columbia, and the Royal Provincial Museum in Victoria, British Columbia, also have large collections with old fragments included. The oldest collection of totem poles in situ are at a World Heritage Site called Ninstints on the Queen Charlotte Islands (Haida Gwaii) of British Columbia, Canada, just southwest of the Alaska Panhandle. They probably date from about the 1850s.

Where is the oldest totem-like art in Alaska? Petroglyph Beach, a state historic park in Wrangell, has the highest concentration of petroglyphs in Southeast Alaska. Petroglyphs are ancient designs or symbols pecked into rocks. Some scholars believe that the figures may be thousands of years old. Identifiable Northwest Coast Indian ovoid, U-shape, and elongated S-shapes are clearly defined. Additional petroglyphs have been discovered on Kodiak Island, at Cape Alitak, in Glacier Bay, at Ground Hog Bay, near Hydaburg Creek on the west coast of Prince of Wales Island, at Hetta Inlet near Sitka, elsewhere on Baranof Island, on Etolin Island, at Anan Creek near Wrangell, at Wrangell, and near Juneau, including Fritz Cove Road, and elsewhere on Douglas Island. The Alaska Historical Preservation Act of 1971 protects all petroglyphs from destruction, defacing, moving, or excavating.

What happens to old totem poles? For the first 50 years of the twentieth century, several methods were pioneered to preserve old totems. Early restoration techniques involved cement, chicken wire, paint, and patches of carved wood. Some tried creosote, glues, and adhesives, or rock salt. No method to replace decayed wood was ever completely satisfactory. Traditionally, outside of Alaska, those that were not taken by museums were allowed to lie where they fell until a relative of the original family that owned the totem could afford to have a new pole created. In Alaska, old poles were replaced by new ones that were not exact copies of the originals but new works of art, possibly with some of the same crests. Occasionally, the totem just decayed and became one with the earth again. From 1850 to 1950, many were collected as soon as they began to tilt. And in the past 50 years, several replicas of old poles have been carved and raised with great ceremony.

What is the connection between the kinship system and totem crests? Ancient Alaskan totem crests originated to define each group's privileges within their traditional tribal kinship systems. Each clan authorized several crests exclusive to them to identify their heritage, rights, and prerogatives. These crests were then emblazoned on many things they owned. Today the Tlingit continue to keep track of their relatives using the old system, the Haida practice a fairly close approximation of their old ways, and the Tsimshian are hosting potlatches to reestablish their old clan affiliations.

What is the relationship between potlatches and totem poles? Traditionally, totem poles were raised as part of a complex ceremony called a potlatch. Both the totem and the potlatch solidified a Native person's kinship and status. Today, a person can commission a totem pole and it is permissible to raise it during its own ceremony, not necessarily as part of a potlatch.

Is it true that there are totem poles spread all over the world? Yes. Because North America's Natives were seen as a "dying people" in the early 1900s, collectors from all over the world scoured the Pacific Northwest and Alaska for masks, regalia, and totem poles. It is possible to see authentic old totems in museums in Australia, Canada, Finland, France, Germany, and many other countries as well as throughout the United States. And in the past half century, commissions for contemporary totems have come from many nations.

Are authentic totem poles still carved? There are excellent carvers alive today who understand the tradition and carve remarkable totems.

How has the totem tradition changed over the years? Some of today's artists are traditionalists, whereas others enjoy stylistic innovation.

Are any of the poles in Alaska's totem parks fake? No, they are not fakes. Some totem park poles are replicas of earlier totems that stood in other locations but have decayed. Others are newly commissioned; still others are restored.

How can a person get an authentic totem carved for him/her? In Haines, Sitka, Ketchikan, and other locations in Alaska, there are master carvers who will consider creating authentic totems for anyone with several thousand dollars as a down payment. Prices go up from there—at approximately $2,000 a foot or more. Famous contemporary carvers such as those mentioned in this book have Web sites.

How long does it take to carve a totem? A totem pole can be carved in about 3 weeks to 3 months, depending on the size of the final pole, and contractual arrangements, and the artist's workload.

Is the "low man on the totem pole" the least important? No. The low man has the same importance as other figures.

Do the "accessories" or poses on totem poles mean anything? The accessories or poses on totems once aided the viewer in interpreting the details of a pole.

How are old crests interpreted on totems today? Because outsiders cannot claim to have the rights to a Native family crest within the old

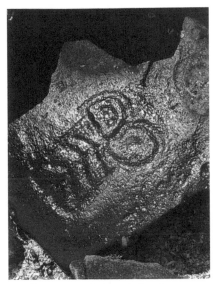

Ancient petroglyphs on the beach near Wrangell are probably thousands of years old.

Alaskan kinship system, some of today's carvers reinterpret old stories searching for links with the new owner's experiences. They sometimes use ancient crest figures within these interpretations. In other cases, they choose emblems they prefer.

Is it true that a slave used to be buried at the base of old totems? No. While this was once claimed to be fact, when hundreds of old totems were dug up in the 1930s and 1940s, no bones were ever found.

Are souvenir totems considered authentic? Native artists began to carve small model poles for sale as souvenirs to tourists more than 100 years ago. If the carver of the totem is skilled and has based the design on the principles of the tradition, it is an authentic totem.

Where can a person learn to carve totem poles in Alaska? A few non-Native people have merited the privilege of becoming an apprentice to an experienced totem carver. Places of learning include Alaska Arts, Inc., in Haines, the Alaska Native Heritage Center in Anchorage, the Totem Heritage Center in Ketchikan, and the Southeast Alaska Indian Cultural Center in Sitka. Classes in general carving and artistic traditions are sponsored by the University of Alaska Southeast.

Where can a person get tools to carve totems? Most carvers make their own tools. Beginners can contact Preferred Edge, www.preferrededge.ca, which has supplied master carvers including Nathan P. Jackson. Also many Alaska carvers use Kestrel Tools available at www.rockisland.com/~kestrel/.

May I ask the author questions about totem poles? Yes. Visit www.totemsnet.com. ∎

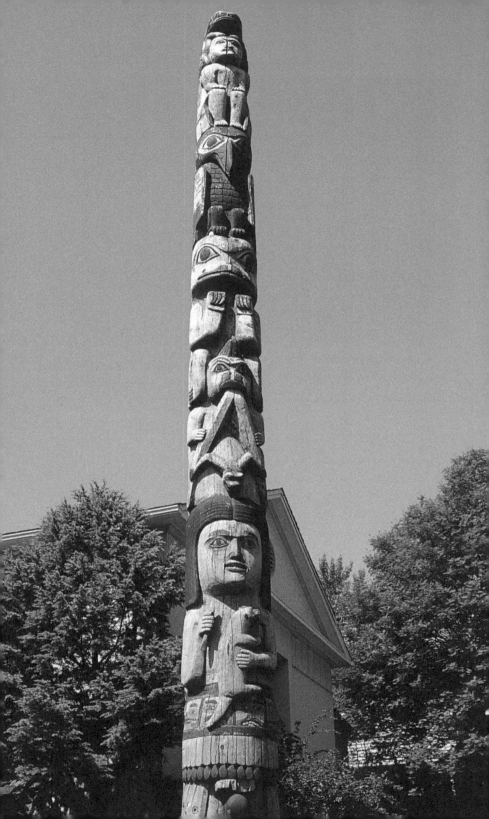

CHAPTER

Visiting Alaska's Totem Poles

Anchorage

Though geographically beyond the range of the Totem People, Anchorage's historic facilities strive to represent a cross-section of Alaska's Native cultures. Though there are few actual totem poles in Anchorage, a fine collection of Native art is permanently exhibited in the International Airport and throughout the downtown area. The few totems that are on public display include two small Tlingit totems at the Alaska Railroad station (411 West First Avenue) and two more at the Alaska State Courthouse (825 West Fourth Avenue). Carved by Lee Wallace (Haida) and Edwin DeWitt (Tlingit), the latter two are called *Attaining a Balance Within.* One depicts how Raven Stole the Sun and the other shows Eagle Boy Stealing Giant Clam. New totems were installed in fall 2004 at the Alaska Native Medical Center (4315 Diplomacy Drive, 907-563-2662). A new pole by Haida artist Donny Varnell can be seen at Ptarmigan Elementary School, 888 Edward Street, Anchorage.

The *Four Story Totem Pole* in Juneau was carved by John Wallace (Haida).
One story involves a woman holding a Land Otter.

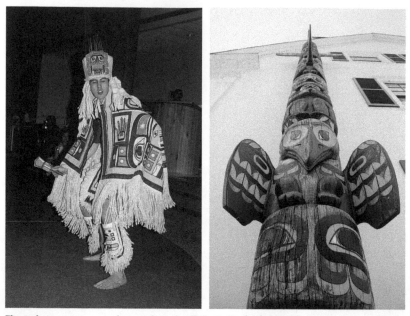

Tlingit dancer wears a modern replica of a Chilkat robe (left). Tlingit creation myth totem pole with Eagle (right) stands next to the Governor's Mansion, Juneau.

The Anchorage Museum of History and Art (121 West Seventh Avenue) features educational programs including classes, tours, lectures, performances, and films. In addition, the museum houses a permanent collection of Native artifacts numbering some 19,500 objects and more than 350,000 historical photographs including many of totem poles. Seven galleries devoted to the "Art of the North" display early paintings of Alaska. The Anchorage Museum currently displays one early Tlingit totem pole on loan from Sitka National Historical Park. It is one of those collected by District Governor John Brady for the Alaska display at the 1904 Louisiana Purchase Centennial Exposition in St. Louis.

Surrounded by the majestic Chugach Mountains, the Alaska Native Heritage Center (8800 Heritage Center Drive) presents an interpretive experience of Alaska's primary indigenous groups, which includes workshops, demonstrations, and guided tours of the indoor exhibits of the center's extensive collections and outdoor village sites.

Angoon

The Tlingit village of Angoon (community association, 907-788-3411), the main settlement on Admiralty Island, is one of the warmest, driest communities in the Southeast. The community, 60 air miles south of Juneau, is served by air taxi and ferry service. The town's culture and traditions are reflected in nine totem poles by Tlingit carvers Wayne Price with Donald Frank as his apprentice and by non-Native carver Ray Peck. Most of the 700-plus residents of Angoon depend on commercial fishing, subsistence hunting, and food gathering. Mysteriously disappearing from Angoon in 1908, a red cedar totem pole dubbed *Totem Teddy* was repatriated in 2003 by members of the *Teikweidi*, or Bear Clan. This totem pole is one of four once displayed in front of a city building, each with a single figure atop a plain shaft and representing major clans of the Angoon Tlingit.

Fairbanks

Although the Interior is well outside the traditional homelands of the Totem People, two poles by Tlingit Amos Wallace are on display in the Alaska and Pioneer Park located on Airport Way. Admission is free to the park, which features special theme areas such as a mining valley, a gold rush town, and a Native village. A pole by Nathan Jackson (Tlingit), Lee Wallace (Haida), and Bert Ryan (Tsimshian) is displayed at the University of Alaska's Museum of the North. A pole by Bert Ryan (Tsimshian) stands at Denali School, 1042 Lathrop Street.

Hoonah

Glacial advances from the years 1400 to about 1750 drove the Glacier Bay Huna people from their homes, across Icy Strait, to Hoonah, "village by the cliff," located on an ice-free natural harbor on Chichagof Island, 40 air miles west of Juneau. Marketing the destination as Port Icy Strait, select cruise lines now stop at this tiny Tlingit village (907-789-1773). Cruise ship visitors now come ashore throughout the summer to see a restored cannery, a few retail outlets, a totem carving hut, and a Native cultural center including a Tlingit dance troupe. The Native village itself, about 2 miles away, is accessible via floatplane or the Alaska ferry system. The ferry stops for an hour so passengers can view four notable totems in this tiny town.

Juneau

The mountain-bound capital city of Alaska is the headquarters for several of the state's most important Native organizations. During the first week of June in even-numbered years, the city of Juneau and the Sealaska Heritage Institute (907-463-4844) host an annual Celebration, featuring thousands of Tlingit, Haida, and Tsimshian people in ceremonial regalia. For everyday visitors, the Juneau Douglas City Museum (Fourth and Main Streets) provides a map for a self-guided walking tour of Juneau's national register of totem poles. Walkers start with the *Harnessing the Atom Totem* ca. 1967, by Amos Wallace (Tlingit) and the *Four Story Totem* ca. 1940 by Hydaburg resident John Wallace (Haida),

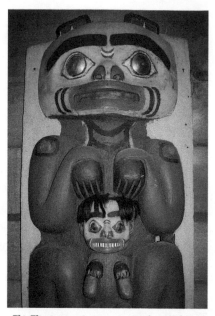

This Tlingit totemic crest carving from Yakutat (circa 1850) depicts a copper-eyed Bear Mother protecting her human-like cub that has shell teeth and hair.

located outside the City Museum (Calhoun and Main Streets). Next comes the *Friendship Totem Pole* by Leo Jacobs (Tlingit)/Alaska Indian Arts, Inc. (Courthouse lobby, Fourth and Seward), the *Waasgo* or *Old Witch Totem* (Main Lobby 8th floor, State Office Building, Fourth & Calhoun St.), carved ca. 1880 by Dwight Wallace (Haida) for the Quit'aas clan. It originally stood in the Haida village of Sukkwan. The *Governor's Totem Pole* (716 Calhoun Street), by Charlie Tagook and William Brown (both Tlingit), reportedly of yellow cedar and carved about 1938, is a creation story with its Mosquito figure attached to the side of the official residence of the governor of Alaska. Next come the *Raven* and *Eagle Totems* (Village Street and Willoughby), carved and painted by Tom Jimmy, Edward Kunz, Edward Kunz Jr., and William Smith (all Tlingit) in 1972, the *Wooshkeetaan* and *Aak'w Tribe* Poles by Nathan Jackson (Tlingit) and Steve Brown, an expert on Northwest Coast formline, (101

Egan Drive). Also within easy walking distance of the downtown is a Native creation myth mural featuring Raven, by Bill C. Ray, (local Juneau artist) found on the City Municipal Building (Marine Park facing Marine Way). The Aak'w Tribe Pole from 1980 by Nathan Jackson (Tlingit) assisted by Steven C. Brown (Tlingit) has been moved indoors to the atrium of the Juneau Douglas High School (1639 Glacier Ave.).

Two Native-owned galleries include the Raven–Eagle Gift Shop (Goldbelt Mount Roberts Tramway) and the Mount Juneau Trading Post (151 Franklin Street). The four-story white building on the corner of Main and Marine Way is the home of the Sealaska Heritage Institute. Visitors are welcome to come inside and view two poles in the lobby by Warren Peale (Tlingit) and Nathan Jackson (Tlingit) plus a canoe, wall screens, and exquisite Chilkat robes. On the fourth floor, exceptional carvings by Jimmy Marks, Ray Peck and Nathan Jackson (all Tlingit) are on display, as well as a 100-year-old Haida button blanket.

A replica of a traditional Tlingit plank house, with elaborate painted *Frog House Posts* and other house posts, screens, and sections of a totem pole from

WHERE IS THE WORLD'S TALLEST TOTEM?

Carved from a single tree and placed on a high bluff, the 132-foot Kake, Alaska, totem pole claims to be the world's tallest, properly dedicated, authentic crest-displaying, single-log totem in the world. It probably is. Built to serve as the Alaska Pavilion centerpiece for Japan's 1970 World's Fair, it was dedicated to all tribes in Southeast Alaska.

Two other taller contenders have lesser credentials. The first is the properly sanctioned 173-foot-high Kwakiutl totem in Alert Bay, B.C., Canada, carved from two or three separate cedar pieces telescoped together. Some say its piecemeal construction disqualifies it. The second is the 149-foot-tall single-piece totem in Kalama, Washington. The Kalama pole was created by a non-Native who adopted the name "Lelooska." The Guinness Book of World Records documents it as the world's tallest totem pole.

And two totems, the world's tallest in their day, are reluctant to give up their claims to being the world's tallest. One, raised in 1956, is Mungo Martin's 127-foot, 7-inch totem in Victoria, B.C.'s, Beacon Hill Park, and the second from the year 1903, now in Tacoma, Washington, at Fireman's Park measures in at a mere 105 feet. ●

Wrangell, can be found at the Alaska State Museum (395 Whittier Street.) This worthwhile museum protects an invaluable ceremonial Frog clan potlatch hat, a Chilkat robe, and a Raven's tail robe (an earlier style of ceremonial garment created with a technique that may have preceded the Chilkat weaving technique), and the top of the original President Lincoln Totem, probably more properly designated as a *First White Man Pole*.

A ride on the Mount Roberts Tramway (490 South Franklin Street) provides an unparalleled view, weather permitting. The trip includes a stop at the Chilkat Theater, where guests see an 18-minute film, view totem-style carvings along the trails, and eat at the Chinook Restaurant. The lower tram terminal features a contemporary totem pole carved by Stephen Jackson (Tlingit). At the top of the tram, Tlingit artist Richard Beasley has carved a series of totemic trail markers on living trees. The House of Wickersham (213 Seventh Street), listed on the National Register of Historic Places, displays an important collection of Native baskets and photographs of early Native culture.

In 1870, the largest permanent Tlingit settlements in the region were Aak'w Villages. In the late 1800s, the village had a row of plank houses and several totem poles. Long since abandoned, only the Auk Village Recreation Site (Glacier Highway, 18 miles north) remains. Before outsiders settled here, clans operated independently within individual territories. Even though all Tlingit people shared language, similar beliefs, and customs, their clans were not united under a rule of one leader or a single governing body. The village site designed by architect Linn Forrest Sr. has one totem pole, the *Yax Te Totem Pole*, dating from the late 1930s, and carved by Frank St. Clair (Tlingit).

Kake

Situated between Juneau and Wrangell, Kake (pronounced CAKE) (village office, 907-785-6471) is home to the world's tallest properly sanctioned totem ca. 1971, measuring 136 feet by various carvers from Alaska Indian Arts, Inc. of Haines including Norman L. Jackson (Tlingit.) In 1990, three new Tlingit totems were raised here at the uppermost tip of Kupreanof Island. And in 1994, for the first potlatch held in Kake in over a century, *Killer Whale Totem* by Norman L. and Mike Jackson (both Tlingit)

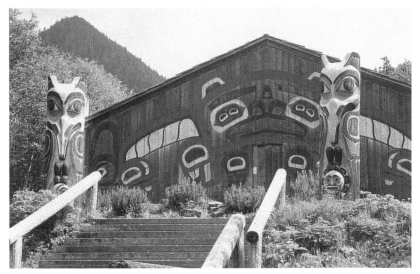

Two Raven totem guards flank the Beaver House, a Tlingit clan house, where visitors can watch Native dancing demonstrations at Saxman Totem Park, Ketchikan.

was raised. Two other newer ten-foot totems from 1994, *Raven* and *Eagle*, by Norman L. Jackson and Mike Jackson (both Tlingit) overlook Little Gunnuk Creek. Occasionally the Keex'Kwaan Tlingit Dancers perform here in traditional regalia.

Ketchikan

For visitors with time for only one totem-viewing stop, Ketchikan is the place to visit. Nearly 70 totem poles stand in this city that occupies former Tlingit territory. Derived from the Kichxaan dialect and meaning "thundering eagle wings," Ketchikan raised the first *Kadjuk Totem* or *Chief Johnson Pole* (Totem Way and Stedman Street) back in 1905. Named for a Tlingit elder Johnson who apparently inherited his position as head of the Ganaxadi in 1902, he had been involved in the 1887 migration of several hundred Tsimshian from Old Metlakatla in BC to New Metlakatla on Annette Island in Alaska. It was Rev. Mather, a Tsimshian and also a carver of the day who wrote that the pole was carved by John Norwlsky, assisted by Billy Dickinson. In the 1940s this totem was among those repaired by the

Civilian Conservation Corps (CCC) project and again riddled with decay, it was taken down in 1982 by the Ketchikan Museum. Replicated by Tlingit carver Israel Shotridge, it was raised again in 1993. Today, this oft-photographed totem stands near its original location. Nearby in tiny Whale Park a centrally located 55-foot pole known as the *Chief Kyan Totem Pole* was also replicated by Israel Shotridge of the Tlingit Brown Bear clan. And an Eagle sculpture, *Thundering Wings*, by Tlingit carver Nathan Jackson, is perched near the dock.

The Westmark Cape Fox Lodge (800 Venetia Way), accessible by funicular tram, is fronted by the *Council of the Clans*—six 12-foot totems by Tlingit carver Lee Wallace. Common areas within the hotel display carved masks and painted house screens as well as silkscreen prints.

The Southeast Alaska Discovery Center (50 Main Street) is just steps from the cruise ships. Operated by the USDA Forest Service, the center's foyer displays three finely executed totems carved in the Haida, Tlingit, and Tsimshian styles carved by Jim Hart (Chief Edenshaw, Haida), Israel Shotridge (Tlingit), and David A. Boxley (Tsimshian), respectively. Inside the Native Traditions Room, visitors can explore a Native fish camp and see traditional wooden implements. Three other relatively new totems by Israel Shotridge (Tlingit,) David A. Boxley (Tsimshian,) and Donald Varnell (Haida) stand at the entrance to the Ketchikan Indian Corporation's Health Clinic.

Authentic Pacific Northwest Coast Indian art is easy to find along bustling Creek Street. Two Native-owned galleries are Hide-A-Way Gifts (18 Creek Street) and Alaska Eagle Arts (5 Creek Street, Suite 3). Outside the Tongass Historical Museum (629 Dock Street) stands *Raven Stealing the Sun* by carver Dempsey Bob (Tlingit). Inside is a small exhibit of Tlingit, Haida, and Tsimshian artifacts.

Listed on the National Register of Historic Places, the Totem Heritage Center (601 Deermont Street) is the storage place for 33 unrestored nineteenth-century totem poles and wood fragments. About 100 years old, they were removed from deserted Tlingit and Haida villages throughout Southeast Alaska. Considered the largest, oldest collection of authentic Alaska totems, the center was established in 1976 to display this irreplaceable collection. Carvers and researchers consider them an important resource. The center also promotes the traditional arts and crafts of the Tlingit, Haida, and

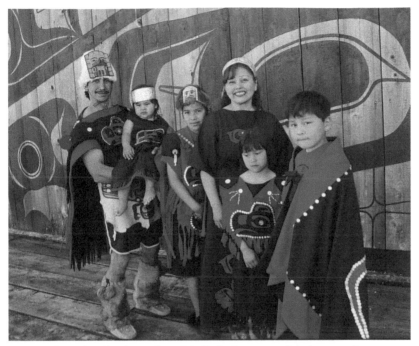

A Tsimshian family, members of the Eagle clan, pose in their dance regalia.

Tsimshian peoples. Nearby there is a self-guided nature trail located beside Ketchikan Creek, across from the Tribal Hatchery and Eagle Center. A new pole by Nathan Jackson (Tlingit) sits in front of the Totem Heritage Center commemorating the center's creation—its founding by several institutions and the tribal elders who authorized the removal of the poles from their original villages.

Fourteen totems and a to-scale Raven Tribal House stand along a trail in the forest at Totem Bight State Park (Milepost 10 North, Tongass Highway). This collection of both Tlingit and Haida totem poles was created in 1938 by Native artists in the CCC. Carved interior house posts symbolize Duk-toothl, a hero wearing a weasel skin hat. The stylized Raven painting on the house and the *Wandering Raven House Entrance Pole* by 1940s-era carver Charles Brown (Tlingit) indicate that the occupants were upper class. On each exterior corner post sits a tattooed potlatch man with a spruce root hat and a "talking stick." Architect Linn Forrest super-vised construction of this model Native village, first called Mud Bight. Workers laid fragments of old poles beside freshly cut cedar logs, and then replicated them. Tools were handmade, modeled on older tools used before the coming of the explorers. Artisans created a natural palette of colors using clamshells, lichen, graphite, copper, pebbles, and salmon eggs. Nature's colors were then simulated with modern paints. At statehood in 1959, title to this important site passed from the federal government to the State of Alaska, and the site was added to the National Register of Historic Places in 1970.

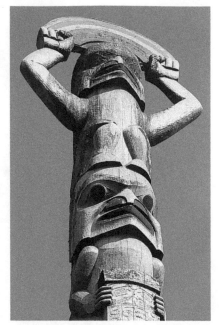

Rainbow Man tops this Tsimshian totem in Metlakatla. He stands on a human holding a "copper," a symbol of wealth and authority.

Saxman Totem Park and Native Village (Milepost 2.5 South) is a pop-ular totem collection in Southeast Alaska. Visitors walk along a dramatic avenue of totem poles up the hill to a gift shop to purchase tickets. Next comes the carving shed, where a carver is often present, and the Beaver clan house, where dancers put on demonstra-tions. The house is a contemporary version of a plank house with a Beaver screen and house posts. Encompassing some 30 totem poles replicated from old Cape Fox villages at Kirk Point, Tongass, Village, and Pennock Islands, each of the totems has a distinctive story to tell. Of special note is a totem depicting a crouching man with a Giant Rock Oyster holding him fast. The Cape Fox Dancers perform here periodically, and carvers are often present to answer questions. Here, Tlingit master carver Nathan P. Jackson and his apprentices produce prestigious totem poles.

Another interesting pole at Saxman is the *Secretary of State Pole*—a classic, rare example of a ridicule pole. It features a likeness of Lincoln's secretary of state, William H. Seward wearing a spruce wood hat and sitting on carved chest. He visited Fort Tongass in 1869 while on a tour of newly purchased Alaska. According to Tlingit tradition, Seward was given gifts and treated royally by the Taantakwaan chiefs, but these honors were not reciprocated, and this pole serves as a reminder of the unpaid debt. Balance and reciprocity remain important concepts in Tlingit society.

Klukwan and Haines

More than 300 years ago, certain Tlingit clans from Prince of Wales Island, the Stikine River valley, the Nass River valley, and Kupreanof Island migrated north and established villages at Klukwan—the Mother Village— and at six other sites. The people of this area came to be known as the Chilkat and the Chilkoot peoples. They carried on an active trade over closely guarded mountain passes with Interior tribes. To keep their routes secret from foreign traders, the Natives would meet ships at the end of the Chilkat Peninsula, far from the grease trails over which they transported guns, iron, tools, blankets, regalia, and eulachon butter. Skilled at traveling in large, oceangoing canoes, the northern Tlingit also traded by sea with more southerly Tlingit people, who in turn traveled as far south as Puget Sound, Washington, and perhaps northern California. A new totem in Haines, the *Wellbriety Kooteeyaa Totem Pole* by Tlingit carver Wayne G. Price, features Raven.

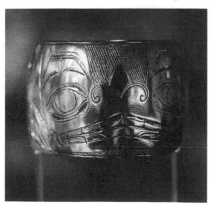

Sailors of the late 1800s introduced Haida carvers to scrimshaw crosshatching.

About 22 miles north of Haines, located adjacent to the Alaska Bald Eagle Preserve, the traditional Tlingit community of Klukwan, located on the north bank of the Chilkat River, is the only remaining ancient village in Alaska. Considered by some as the citadel of Tlingit art, it is known for its Chilkat blankets and dance robes traditionally woven from mountain goat hair and cedar bark. The village is currently developing a Cultural Heritage Center and Museum.

In 1881, Chilkat Indians from the now-abandoned village of Yandestaki, negotiating with Presbyterian minister Dr. Sheldon Jackson, ceremonially received Jackson's friend, S. Hall Young, who was to build a mission and school. The site chosen was known as Dei shu, "the end of the trail." There were as yet no buildings on the site that was later to become the town of Haines. Rev. Eugene Willard and his wife, Caroline, soon arrived to carry on the missionary work. The mission was renamed Haines in 1884 in honor of Mrs. F. E. Haines, who chaired

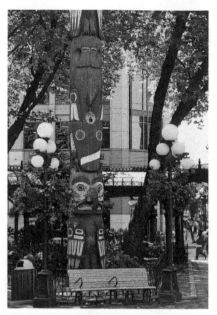

The Tlingit Goodwill Pole in Seattle's Pioneer Square has a storied history.

the National Committee that had raised funds for the mission's construction. Canneries started up in the area, prospectors traveled through on their way to the ancient trade routes over the Chilkoot and White Passes, and with the advent of the gold rush, many newcomers arrived. The town of Haines grew up around the mission site, and Fort Seward was built nearby.

Today Chilkat blankets and a replica of Tlingit slatted wooden armor as well as Russian trade goods are on display at the Sheldon Museum and Cultural Center (Main and First Street).

Fort William H. Seward welcomes visitors to view Alaskan artists and carvers at their work, including totem carving, silkscreen making, and silver carving. Workshops are sometimes available for those who would like to learn totem pole carving alongside master carvers (Alaska Indian Arts, Hospital Building 13, Fort Seward.) The facility includes officers' headquarters, barracks, a tribal house, a trapper's cabin, and a cache (a structure on stilts to protect food from bears and other critters.)

Starting from the town of Haines, local tours by appointment (907) 767-5770 take in the Chilkat Bald Eagle Reserve, the Chilkat River, Native tribal house interiors, Eagle and Raven clan wall screens, and totem poles. Participants may sometimes taste Native fry bread and learn how the Tlingit render eulachon fish into "Indian butter."

Haines displays several totem poles—all carved by various Tlingit artists and their apprentices. For specific directions to each of the totems stop in at Alaska Indian Arts, 24 Fort Seward Drive, a local museum. The totems are located in and around the townsite: a *Raven Pole* and an *Eagle Pole* (at the Mile 1 Welcome Sign); an outside *Raven Pole* and an inside *Raven Pole* (at Chilkat Center on Tower Road); a totem representing the *Folletti Family* (at Chilkat Valley Arts on 209 Willard St.); a tall *Friendship Pole* (at Haines Elementary School on Main Street); a *Killer Whale Pole* (at the Haines Firehall at 0.5 mile on the Haines Highway); a pole with *Jonico and Koostaka* (at a residence on 26 Fort Seward Drive); an *Eagle Clan Pole* (at Lookout Park on Front Street); a *Friendship Totem* (at the Sheldon Museum at 10 First Ave S.); a *Raven Pole* (at a residence on 524 Main Street); and four totems representing the area's clans at the Tribal House on the Fort Seward Parade Grounds. Also inside the tribal house are a *Beaver Pole*, a *Raven/Whale Pole*, and a *Raven/Frog Pole.*

Metlakatla

Today, about 1,200 Tsimshian people live in Metlakatla on Annette Island, Alaska's only Indian reservation and only Tsimshian village, about 8 oceangoing miles south of Ketchikan. Several old Tlingit totems were standing on the beach when 823 Tsimshian from Canada arrived on August 7, 1887. Missionary William Duncan had negotiated with President Grover Cleveland to secure the entire expanse of Annette Island for them to settle. Enforcing strict rules against alcohol and cleaning up the village to his exacting Victorian standards, Duncan respected Tsimshian traditions but felt that totem carving was a waste of time. Against the backdrop of this philosophy, most of the original totems were destroyed, though two were shipped to Sheldon Jackson's museum in Sitka.

Starting in the 1970s, several villagers dedicated themselves to becoming culture bearers and relearning their forgotten traditions. A dance troupe was formed and young men began carving as apprentices. After much study, carver David A. Boxley (Tsimshian) raised the first Metlakatla totem in 1982. During the next 15 years, he and his son David R. Boxley (Tsimshian), along with noted carver Wayne Hewson (Tsimshian), created more than 42 poles and numerous art pieces. Among them, they carved 11 of the 13 totems now standing in Metlakatla. Private or group guided tours of Metlakatla village, including Rev. Duncan's Cottage and the town totem poles, are available through Pat Beal, Tourism Director, 907-886-8687. In summer, the residents staff a small craft market that is open when visitors are in town.

Prince of Wales Island

Of the approximately 1,800 Haida people now residing in Alaska, about 300 live on Prince of Wales Island. During the late 1600s, a group of Haida migrated to this enormous island from British Columbia's Queen Charlotte Islands. The break-away subgroup, generally known as the Kaigani Haida, discovered abundant resources and several abandoned Tlingit villages. There they built their own clan houses and added their own totem poles.

Today their descendants live in the small villages of Craig and Klawock, about 7 miles apart, and in Hydaburg, 30 miles from Craig. In Craig there is

SEATTLE'S GOODWILL TOTEM

Goodwill has many shades of meaning, but rarely rises to such ironic levels. In 1899, a goodwill mission traveled to Alaska to celebrate Seattle's lucrative links with that gold-producing region. While cruising home on the steamship City of Seattle, and reportedly well fortified with intoxicants, the delegates spotted a fine Tlingit totem pole near Port Tongass, Alaska. Thinking the seaside village abandoned, crewmen rowed ashore, cut down the pole, and loaded it aboard before steaming away. Returning to their village, residents were stunned at the pilfering, protested through letters, then sent delegations south to Seattle.

The totem, raised in a well-publicized civic ceremony, stayed put—though in due course, the perpetrators paid a small fine for their transgression. In 1938, an arsonist set the pole aflame, and in 1941, as part of the CCC program, descendants of the villagers were paid to replicate it. As a gesture of goodwill, they officially presented the storied totem to the city. Seattle restored the Tlingit totem pole standing in Pioneer Square once again in 1972, and five years later had it declared a National Landmark. ●

a small Haida totem park on the waterfront, and Klawock has a totem park with totem poles listed on the National Register of Historic Places. Klawock raised seven new totem poles in 2005. The final Raven Clan Pole rose under the careful eye of carver Jon Rowan (Haida) and his crew of young apprentices. Rowan, who teaches Native arts at Klawock city schools, carved all seven of the replica poles with the help of his students. One is Girl with a Woodworm Totem. Some of the totems are original and some were replicated from the previously occupied village of Tuxekan, an abandoned Tlingit village on the northern half of Prince of Wales Island. In the 1930s, the Civilian Conservation Corps and the US Forest Service brought 21 totem poles to Hydaburg, five of which were restored. The remaining 16 poles were replicated between 1939 and 1942 under the direction of Haida carver John Wallace. Many are in need of restoration once again. At the school there are 10 Haida totems of more recent vintage, and nearby there is a new Wellness Totem by Wayne Price (Tlingit) with three Watchmen on top.

In Kasaan, the Totems Historic District consists of *Chief Son-I-Hat's Whale House* and *Frontal Pole*, with eight additional poles that are either restored originals or copies of the original poles from the Old Kasaan village site. The park was established in the late 1930s as part of the CCC project. In 2008, the park received a grant to develop a plan for restoring *Chief Son-I-Hat's Whale House.*

Seattle, Washington

Seattle is also a good place to view Alaska totems. With its long history as a staging stop on the way to and from Alaska, Seattle's collectors, tourists, missionaries, gold miners, traders, and trappers were some of the first outsiders to acquire and sell Alaskan Native arts and crafts more than a century ago. Alaska's fishing fleet still berths in Seattle, and the city continues to supply various Alaskan needs and vice versa.

Twin totems carved by Quinault artist Marvin Oliver and James Bender stand near the Pike Place Market at Victor Steinbrueck Park. The most famous totem landmark in Seattle is nearby: the *Goodwill Pole* in Pioneer Square. On October 18, 1899, a 60-foot totem pole taken from the Tlingit village of Fort Tongass, Alaska, was unveiled in Seattle's Pioneer Square. On October 22, 1938, an arsonist seriously damaged it, and in 1940 it was replaced with a replica carved by the Tlingit descendants of the carvers of the original totem. On this complex totem, Alaska's major emblems are represented: Raven, Bear, Eagle, Killer Whale, and Wolf. Several downtown Seattle galleries specialize in Northwest Coast Indian art and represent notable Pacific Northwest and Southeast Alaska Native artists.

The Burke Museum (University of Washington, 17th Avenue NE and NE 45th Street) often features a Northwest Coast master carver in attendance several days a week working on a totem pole or major wood item such as a mask. Near the entrance are three replica totems by master carver and historian Bill Holm. These include a replicated Haida house front pole, first carved in the 1870s, and a Tsimshian memorial pole from the 1880s. Standing nearby, a totemic Killer Whale sculpture, *Single Fin*, from the abandoned village of Howkan, on Prince of Wales Island, was replicated from a nineteenth-century Haida grave marker.

At the turn of the twentieth century, collector John H. Hauberg brought back many articles from Alaska's Tlingit and Haida cultures, now on display at the Seattle Art Museum (100 University Street). In 1991, the museum acquired the John H. Hauberg Collection, including almost 200 Native American masks, sculptures, textiles, and decorative and household objects from the Pacific Northwest Coast up to Alaska.

There are some brightly painted totem poles at the Daybreak Star Indian Cultural Center (Discovery Park, West Government Way at 36th Avenue). And the Tillicum Village Tour (starts at Piers 55 and 56) takes visitors on a boat ride to nearby Blake Island, where a barbecue salmon dinner is served in a model clan house while Northwest Native dancers perform.

Sitka

Built on the site of an ancient Tlingit village, in the shelter of Baranof Island and the shadow of volcanic Mount Edgecumbe, Sitka is located in a particularly striking setting. Its Tlingit names were *Sheet Ka* and *Shee Atika*, meaning "the village behind the islands." Sitka's unique Tlingit, Aleut, and Russian heritage combine in interesting ways throughout this university town. The Sitka Tribe of Alaska Community House (200 Katlian Street) offers periodic presentations of Native dances, as well as seasonal walking or bus tours of the town, and features house front and interior screens and house posts by Will Burkhart (Tlingit). To see cere-monial Chilkat Raven's tail robes periodically in the making and the works of over 100 Alaska artists, drop into the Sitka Rose Gallery (419 Lincoln Street).

In the 1890s, Rev. Dr. Sheldon Jackson, a Presbyterian missionary, acquired nearly 5,000 traditional items including dozens of carvings of argillite, a soft black slate favored by Haida carvers. His collection, includ-ing four historic totem poles, can be viewed at the Sheldon Jackson Museum (104 College Drive.)

Totem seekers must see the combined Sitka National Historical Park (103 Monastery Street) and Southeast Alaska Indian Cultural Center (106 Metlakatla Street). Located on traditional Kiks.ádi land and first set aside as a park in 1890 by President Benjamin Harrison, the site includes 15

THE SHAKES DYNASTY

A piece of Wrangell history, the title "Shakes," also spelled "Shaikes," was origi-nally conferred upon one Tlingit Chief Gushklin. About the year 1700, after a victory against the Nisga'a and Skeena River Tsimshian tribes in British Columbia, Gushklin accepted the tribute of his enemy's defeated chief. Rather than submit to the degradation of being a slave, the prisoner

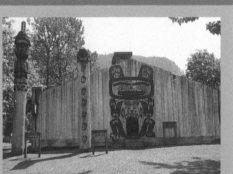

The Shakes dynasty Tlingit clan house was restored by the Civilian Conservation Corps in the 1930s and stands on an island in Wrangell.

removed his Killer Whale hat, and granted the victor his own name—We-Shakes, later shortened to "Shakes." Shakes I was soon succeeded by his eldest nephew, then his brother. The reign of Ka-shishk, or Shakes III, is remembered for his benevolence. Disguising himself in plain clothes, he discovered that his people were tired of the hardships of war. His long reign ended when, aged and blind, he was killed by a falling tree. Many slaves were sacrificed at his funeral. ➤

restored poles in a serene section of temperate rain forest with 2 miles of wooded pathways. Some were copied from a Haida village on Prince of Wales Island; others are from the local Tlingit tradition. The latter include *K'alyaan, Wolf, Frog/Raven, Trader Legend, Raven Memorial, Mosquito Legend,* and *Raven/Shark Poles.* John Brady, governor of the Alaska Territory from 1897 to 1906, brought the original collection of totems to this spot. The remains of this original collection are displayed in a new wing of the Visitor Center. The park's Visitor Center features exhibits on Tlingit culture and a slide program on the 1804 Battle of Sitka. A wing houses the Southeast Alaska Indian Cultural Center, an independent organization of Tlingit artists who demonstrate traditional wood and silver carving during various hours in tourist season. In front of the center stands the 35-foot *Haa leelk'u has Kaa sta heeni deiy,* by Will Burkhart, Wayne Price, and Tommy Joseph (all Tlingit), which is a multiclan pole commemorating the Kaagwaantaan, Kiks.ádi, and Coho clans—the three Tlingit-speaking groups who lived in the area before the Russians arrived. Several other

THE SHAKES DYNASTY continued

His nephew, Shawt-shugo-ish or Shakes IV, was reputedly the first of the Nan-yan-yi chieftains to see a white man—a trader. A receptacle in the back of a Grizzly Bear totem holds Shawt-shugo-ish's ashes. Kow-ish-te, his nephew, became Shakes V. During his tenure, in 1840, the Russian Fort Dionysius was transferred to Britain's Hudson's Bay Company and renamed Fort Stikine. When the Americans purchased Alaska in 1867, the fort was renamed yet again to Fort Wrangell. Chief Shakes V thus witnessed Russian, British, and finally American occupation—all within his lifetime. A Russian-design wood fence surmounted by two replicated Killer Whales enclose his remains. The Whale originals are displayed in his house. Gush-klin II became Shakes VI, and the Chief Shakes Tribal House, built in 1939 through the auspices of the CCC, was his. Throughout their fortunate lifetimes, through their many potlatches, this dynasty acquired an extraordinary number of traditional goods. These include a dozen totem poles that are often photographed by those visiting his house in Wrangell. Old faded postcards of Shakes's totems, dugout canoe, and clan house are frequently sold through Internet auction sites. ●

relatively new poles in the park, including the *K'alyaan Pole* by Tommy Joseph and Fred Beltran (Tlingit), are placed on the site of the Kiks.ádi clan's fort used during their 1804 battle with the Russians.

Wrangell

Situated at the mouth of the Stikine River, Wrangell (pronounced RANG-ul) is home to the Tlingit who arrived here about 1,000 years ago and proceeded to dominate commerce in the area. About 1870, thousands of scruffy miners began to appear on their ancient grease trails, searching for gold. Schools and missions followed, and in the 1930s the Bureau of Indian Affairs brought Native people from all over Alaska here for job training.

The town's major attraction is the restored Chief Shakes Tribal House of the Bear (Front Street, 907-874-2023), which is surrounded by rustling cottonwood trees and a dozen historically important Tlingit totem poles, including *Double Killer Whale Crest Hat Totem* and *Grizzly Bear Mortuary Totem*. An interpreter periodically provides the history of the house interior, while visitors view the magnificent *Frog House Posts* of the Kiks.ádi clan. The Stikine elders also maintain several Tlingit totems at nearby Kiks'Adi Totem Park. These include the *Killisnoo Beaver, Double Raven*, and the *One-Legged Fisherman Pole* also known as the *Blind Fisherman*.

A new Wrangell Museum opened in 2004 (296 Outer Drive) to safeguard four finely carved Tlingit houseposts originating from about 1740, and thought to be the oldest in existence. The carvings are supplemented by a collection of spruce root and cedar bark baskets from the turn of the twentieth century, a spruce canoe—one of few in existence—and a collection of Tlingit masks.

Some of the best surviving examples of ancient Native artistic expression are petroglyphs, or rock carvings, found on boulders along the shore throughout Alaska. Petroglyph Beach near Wrangell has the highest concentration of such petroglyphs in Southeast, and has been designated a State Historic Park. There is a wheelchair-accessible boardwalk to a deck overlooking the beach, the Stikine River, and Zimovia Strait. Replicas of several petroglyph designs are displayed on the deck, and visitors who bring some paper and crayons may make rubbings of some of the etched figures. ∎

FURTHER READING

Sources

Barbeau, Marius. *Totem Poles*. Ottawa, Ontario: King's Printer, 1950.

Boas, Franz. "Mythology and folk-tales of the North American Indians." *Journal of American Folklore* 27(106):374–410, October-December 1914.

——. *Primitive Art* (1927). Irvington-on-Hudson, New York: Capitol Publishing Company, 1951.

Brown, Steven C. (text), and Paul Macapia (photographs). *Native Visions: Evolution in Northwest Coast Art from the Eighteenth Through the Twentieth Century*. Seattle: Seattle Art Museum in association with the University of Washington Press, 1998.

Emmons, George Thornton, and Frederica de Laguna. *The Tlingit Indians*. Seattle: University of Washington Press, 1991.

Fedje, Daryl W., and Rolf W. Mathewes. "Haida Gwaii: Human history and environment from the time of the Loon to the time of the Iron People." *Journal of Island and Coastal Archaeology* 2(2):281–83, July 2007.

Fleurieu, Charles Pierre Claret. *A Voyage Round the World 1790–1792*. Performed by Etienne Marchand. Translated from the French by N. Israel. New York: Da Capo Press, 1970.

Garfield, Viola E., and Linn A. Forest. *The Wolf and the Raven: Totem Poles of Southeastern Alaska*. Seattle: University of Washington Press, 1948.

Holm, Bill. *Northwest Coast Indian Art: An Analysis of Form*. Seattle: University of Washington Press, 1965.

National Park Service. *Carved History: The Totem Poles and House Posts of Sitka National Historical Park*. Anchorage: Alaska Natural History Association, 2000.

Swann, Brian, ed. *Voices from Four Directions: Contemporary Translations of the Native Literatures of North America*. Lincoln: University of Nebraska Press, 2004.

Swanton, John R. *Contributions to the Ethnology of the Haida*. Publications of the Jesup North Pacific Expedition 5(1), American Museum of Natural History Memoirs 8(1). New York: G. E. Stechert, 1905.

——. *Haida Texts and Myths: Skidegate Dialect*. Bureau of American Ethnology Bulletin 29. Washington, D.C.: Government Printing Office, 1905.

——. *Tlingit Myths and Texts*. Washington, D.C.: Smithsonian Institution, 1909.

Suggested Reading

Langdon, Steve J. *The Native People of Alaska*. Anchorage: Greatland Graphics, 1993.

Shearar, Cheryl. *Understanding Northwest Coast Art: A Guide to Crests, Beings, and Symbols*. 5th edition. Seattle: University of Washington Press, 2003.

Smelcer, John E. *The Raven and the Totem*. Anchorage, Alaska: A Salmon Run Book, 1992.

Stewart, Hilary. *Looking at Indian Art of the Northwest Coast*. Seattle: University of Washington Press, 1979.

Wright, Robin Kathleen. *Northern Haida Master Carvers*. Seattle: University of Washington Press, 2001.

Index

9 780882 407319